The Best of Betjeman

The Best of Betjeman

Selected by John Guest

BOOK CLUB ASSOCIATES
LONDON

Published in association with
Penguin Books Ltd

The Acknowledgements on page 11
constitute an extension of this copyright page

Printed in Great Britain by
Cox & Wyman Ltd,
London, Fakenham and Reading

0 7195 3555 7

This edition published 1979 by
Book Club Associates
By arrangement with John Murray Ltd.

Contents

Contents

Part Three   Metro-land

Editor's Note

There is one obvious omission from the poetry selected for this book: I have not quoted from *Summoned by Bells*. This blank-verse autobiographical poem is more than a hundred pages long, and is inevitably more relaxed in style than the shorter poems. I have been limited for space, and to have included passages that adequately represented the mood and manner of *Summoned by Bells* would have entailed the elimination of a number of shorter poems. I can only urge readers to obtain *Summoned by Bells* and to read it in its entirety.

There was an earlier volume of Sir John Betjeman's essays and radio talks – mostly on topographical and architectural subjects – selected by Mrs John Piper and published in 1952 under the title, *First and Last Loves*. To this I am indebted for four pieces in the selection that follows.

Nearly half a century has passed since the appearance in the *London Mercury* of the first prose item in this book, 'Lord Mount Prospect'. Publication dates have therefore been supplied throughout so that the poems and passages of prose may be read in the light, as it were, of their various decades.

I make no apology for including in Part Two what may appear to be a rather big selection from one source, the Introduction to *English Parish Churches* (Collins, 1958). This essay, half the length of a book in itself, is of great importance in the body of Sir John's prose writings. And, on a lesser matter, I make no apology for including the piece on Theo Marzials. Readers may feel that it contains as much quotation as original Betjeman; it does, but the pleasure it gives as a whole justifies, I hope, its inclusion here.

To the great number of readers who for many years have enjoyed Sir John's poetry, essays and radio talks, there has recently been added a vast new public through the medium of television. As a script writer and as a visible narrator, he has proved himself 'a natural' in this relatively new field. I have therefore thought it valid to include one of his television film scripts – a slightly abbreviated version of 'Metro-land'. But it must be said that 'Metro-land', and a number of other television films for which Sir John has written the scripts, are the result of team-work, both in the conception and in the making of the film. Edward Mirzoeff, the producer, Edward Roberts, the film editor, and Sir John as writer and narrator, work almost as closely together as a musical trio. I am grateful to Mr Mirzoeff and to Mr Roberts for much information and for the time they gave me. I must also thank Mr Marshall Cubbon of the Manx National Museum; Miss Hermione Hobhouse, Secretary of the Victorian Society; Mr John Murray, Sir John's publisher; Miss Jenny Prior; Mr Christopher Young; and, not least, Miss Challice B. Reed and Miss Barbara Varley of the BBC Script Library. Finally, my thanks to Sir John himself. His good humour and patience with my innumerable queries seemed inexhaustible.

J.G.

Sources and Acknowledgements

All the poems in Part One with the exception of the last two, 'Chelsea 1977' and 'Summer', are taken from the volumes given in the list of Contents, all published by John Murray. 'Chelsea 1977' was published in *Hand and Eye*, 1977, a volume in honour of Sir Sacheverell Sitwell, edited by Geoffrey Elborn and published by the Tragara Press, Edinburgh, to whom acknowledgement is made. 'Summer' is taken from *A Dragon Century 1877–1977*, edited by C. H. Jaques. 'Chelsea 1977' and 'Summer' both appear by kind permission of the author.

In Part Two, Prose, each item is individually dated for reasons given in the Editor's Note. 'Blisland', 'Bournemouth', 'St Endellion' and 'Highworth' were published in *First and Last Loves*, 1952; but since these essays were originally written as BBC talks, the dates given in the list of Contents are those on which they were first broadcast. There are, incidentally, minor differences between the original BBC scripts and the texts as published; in each case the text followed is that printed in *First and Last Loves*. 'Early English' is reprinted from *A Pictorial History of English Architecture*, 1972; and 'St Pancras' from *London's Historic Railway Stations*, 1972, all published by John Murray. 'A Letter' carries an explanatory note in the text.

The remaining prose items in Part Two are included by kind permission of the author and the following publishers: Victor Gollancz for 'Lord Mount Prospect' from *Great Stories of Detection, Mystery and Horror*, 1934, ('Lord Mount Prospect' first appeared in the *London Mercury*, 1929); EP Publishing Ltd for 'Motopolis' and 'An Approach to Oxford' from *An Oxford University Chest*, 1970 (first published by John Miles, London, 1938); Dennis Dobson Ltd for 'The Isle of Man' from *Portraits of Islands*, edited by Eileen Molony, 1951; William Collins Ltd for passages from the Introduction to *Collins Pocket Guide to English Parish Churches*, 1958; the *Daily Telegraph* Weekend Magazine, 12 August 1963, for

'Middlesex'; Shell-Mex and BP Ltd for 'Cornwall', an edited version of the Introduction to *Cornwall, A Shell Guide*, 1964; and, finally, the BBC for 'Theo Marzials', 1950, 'Kelmscott', 1952; and 'Metro-land', 1973, which, in a slightly abbreviated form, comprises Part Three of this selection.

Part One · Poems

Death in Leamington

She died in the upstairs bedroom
  By the light of the ev'ning star
That shone through the plate glass window
  From over Leamington Spa.

Beside her the lonely crochet
  Lay patiently and unstirred,
But the fingers that would have work'd it
  Were dead as the spoken word.

And Nurse came in with the tea-things
  Breast high 'mid the stands and chairs –
But Nurse was alone with her own little soul,
  And the things were alone with theirs.

She bolted the big round window,
  She let the blinds unroll,
She set a match to the mantle,
  She covered the fire with coal.

And 'Tea!' she said in a tiny voice
  'Wake up! It's nearly *five*.'
Oh! Chintzy, chintzy cheeriness,
  Half dead and half alive!

Do you know that the stucco is peeling?
  Do you know that the heart will stop?
From those yellow Italianate arches
  Do you hear the plaster drop?

Nurse looked at the silent bedstead,
   At the grey, decaying face,
As the calm of a Leamington ev'ning
   Drifted into the place.

She moved the table of bottles
   Away from the bed to the wall;
And tiptoeing gently over the stairs
   Turned down the gas in the hall.

Hymn

The Church's Restoration
  In eighteen-eighty-three
Has left for contemplation
  Not what there used to be.
How well the ancient woodwork
  Looks round the Rect'ry hall,
Memorial of the good work
  Of him who plann'd it all.

He who took down the pew-ends
  And sold them anywhere
But kindly spared a few ends
  Work'd up into a chair.
O worthy persecution
  Of dust! O hue divine!
O cheerful substitution,
  Thou varnishéd pitch-pine!

Church furnishing! Church furnishing!
  Sing art and crafty praise!
He gave the brass for burnishing
  He gave the thick red baize,
He gave the new addition,
  Pull'd down the dull old aisle,
– To pave the sweet transition
  He gave th' encaustic tile.

Of marble brown and veinéd
  He did the pulpit make;
He order'd windows stainéd
  Light red and crimson lake.

Sing on, with hymns uproarious,
    Ye humble and aloof,
Look up! and oh how glorious
    He has restored the roof!

Westgate-on-Sea

Hark, I hear the bells of Westgate,
  I will tell you what they sigh,
Where those minarets and steeples
  Prick the open Thanet sky.

Happy bells of eighteen-ninety,
  Bursting from your freestone tower!
Recalling laurel, shrubs and privet,
  Red geraniums in flower.

Feet that scamper on the asphalt
  Through the Borough Council grass,
Till they hide inside the shelter
  Bright with ironwork and glass,

Striving chains of ordered children
  Purple by the sea-breeze made,
Striving on to prunes and suet
  Past the shops on the Parade.

Some with wire around their glasses,
  Some with wire across their teeth,
Writhing frames for running noses
  And the drooping lip beneath.

Church of England bells of Westgate!
  On this balcony I stand,
White the woodwork wriggles round me,
  Clock towers rise on either hand.

For me in my timber arbour
   You have one more message yet,
'Plimsolls, plimsolls in the summer,
    Oh goloshes in the wet!'

The Wykehamist

(To Randolph Churchill, but not about him.)

Broad of Church and broad of mind,
Broad before and broad behind,
A keen ecclesiologist,
A rather dirty Wykehamist.
'Tis not for us to wonder why
He wears that curious knitted tie;
We should not cast reflections on
The very slightest kind of don.
We should not giggle as we like
At his appearance on his bike;
It's something to become a bore,
And more than that, at twenty-four.
It's something too to know your wants
And go full pelt for Norman fonts.
Just now the chestnut trees are dark
And full with shadow in the park,
And 'six o'clock!' St Mary calls
Above the mellow college walls.
The evening stretches arms to twist
And captivate her Wykehamist.
But not for him these autumn days,
He shuts them out with heavy baize;
He gives his Ovaltine a stir
And nibbles at a 'petit beurre',
And, satisfying fleshly wants,
He settles down to Norman fonts.

The Arrest of Oscar Wilde
at the Cadogan Hotel

He sipped at a weak hock and seltzer
  As he gazed at the London skies
Through the Nottingham lace of the curtains
  Or was it his bees-winged eyes?

To the right and before him Pont Street
  Did tower in her new built red,
As hard as the morning gaslight
  That shone on his unmade bed.

'I want some more hock in my seltzer,
  And Robbie, please give me your hand –
Is this the end or beginning?
  How can I understand?

'So you've brought me the latest *Yellow Book*:
  And Buchan has got in it now:
Approval of what is approved of
  Is as false as a well-kept vow.

'More hock, Robbie – where is the seltzer?
  Dear boy, pull again at the bell!
They are all little better than *cretins*,
  Though this *is* the Cadogan Hotel.

'One astrakhan coat is at Willis's –
  Another one's at the Savoy:
Do fetch my morocco portmanteau,
  And bring them on later, dear boy.'

A thump, and a murmur of voices –
   ('Oh why must they make such a din?')
As the door of the bedroom swung open
   And TWO PLAIN CLOTHES POLICEMEN came in:

'Mr Woilde, we 'ave come for tew take yew
   Where felons and criminals dwell:
We must ask yew tew leave with us quoietly
   For this *is* the Cadogan Hotel.'

He rose, and he put down *The Yellow Book.*
   He staggered – and, terrible-eyed,
He brushed past the palms on the staircase
   And was helped to a hansom outside.

Slough

Come, friendly bombs, and fall on Slough
It isn't fit for humans now,
There isn't grass to graze a cow
   Swarm over, Death!

Come, bombs, and blow to smithereens
Those air-conditioned, bright canteens,
Tinned fruit, tinned meat, tinned milk, tinned beans
   Tinned minds, tinned breath.

Mess up the mess they call a town –
A house for ninety-seven down
And once a week a half-a-crown
   For twenty years,

And get that man with double chin
Who'll always cheat and always win,
Who washes his repulsive skin
   In women's tears,

And smash his desk of polished oak
And smash his hands so used to stroke
And stop his boring dirty joke
   And make him yell.

But spare the bald young clerks who add
The profits of the stinking cad;
It's not their fault that they are mad,
   They've tasted Hell.

It's not their fault they do not know
The birdsong from the radio,
It's not their fault they often go
    To Maidenhead

And talk of sports and makes of cars
In various bogus Tudor bars
And daren't look up and see the stars
    But belch instead.

In labour-saving homes, with care
Their wives frizz out peroxide hair
And dry it in synthetic air
    And paint their nails.

Come, friendly bombs, and fall on Slough
To get it ready for the plough.
The cabbages are coming now;
    The earth exhales.

Love in a Valley

Take me, Lieutenant, to that Surrey homestead!
  Red comes the winter and your rakish car,
Red among the hawthorns, redder than the hawberries
  And trails of old man's nuisance, and noisier far.
Far, far below me roll the Coulsdon woodlands,
  White down the valley curves the living rail,
Tall, tall, above me, olive spike the pinewoods,
  Olive against blue-black, moving in the gale.

Deep down the drive go the cushioned rhododendrons,
  Deep down, sand deep, drives the heather root,
Deep the spliced timber barked around the summer-house,
  Light lies the tennis-court, plantain underfoot.
What a winter welcome to what a Surrey homestead!
  Oh! the metal lantern and white enamelled door!
Oh! the spread of orange from the gas-fire on the carpet!
  Oh! the tiny patter, sandalled footsteps on the floor!

Fling wide the curtains! – that's a Surrey sunset
  Low down the line sings the Addiscombe train,
Leaded are the windows lozenging the crimson,
  Drained dark the pines in resin-scented rain.
Portable Lieutenant! they carry you to China
  And me to lonely shopping in a brilliant arcade:
Firm hand, fond hand, switch the giddy engine!
  So for us a last time is bright light made.

Dorset

Rime Intrinsica, Fontmell Magna, Sturminster Newton and
Melbury Bubb,
Whist upon whist upon whist upon whist drive, in Institute, Legion
and Social Club.
Horny hands that hold the aces which this morning held the plough –
While Tranter Reuben, T. S. Eliot, H. G. Wells and Edith Sitwell
lie in Mellstock Churchyard now.

Lord's Day bells from Bingham's Melcombe, Iwerne Minster,
Shroton, Plush,
Down the grass between the beeches, mellow in the evening hush.
Gloved the hands that hold the hymn-book, which this morning
milked the cow –
While Tranter Reuben, Mary Borden, Brian Howard and Harold
Acton lie in Mellstock Churchyard now.

Light's abode, celestial Salem! Lamps of evening, smelling strong,
Gleaming on the pitch-pine, waiting, almost empty evensong:
From the aisles each window smiles on grave and grass and
yew-tree bough –
While Tranter Reuben, Gordon Selfridge, Edna Best and Thomas
Hardy lie in Mellstock Churchyard now.

NOTE: *The names in the last lines of these stanzas are put in not out of
malice or satire but merely for their euphony.*

Death of King George V

'New King arrives in his capital by air...'
Daily Newspaper

Spirits of well-shot woodcock, partridge, snipe
  Flutter and bear him up the Norfolk sky:
In that red house in a red mahogany book-case
  The stamp collection waits with mounts long dry.

The big blue eyes are shut which saw wrong clothing
  And favourite fields and coverts from a horse;
Old men in country houses hear clocks ticking
  Over thick carpets with a deadened force;

Old men who never cheated, never doubted,
  Communicated monthly, sit and stare
At the new suburb stretched beyond the run-way
  Where a young man lands hatless from the air.

A Shropshire Lad

N.B. This should be recited with a Midland accent. Captain Webb, the swimmer and a relation of Mary Webb by marriage, was born at Dawley in an industrial district in Salop.

The gas was on in the Institute,*
   The flare was up in the gym,
A man was running a mineral line,
   A lass was singing a hymn,
When Captain Webb the Dawley man,
   Captain Webb from Dawley,
Came swimming along in the old canal
   That carried the bricks to Lawley.
       Swimming along –
       Swimming along –
       Swimming along from Severn,
And paying a call at Dawley Bank while swimming along to Heaven.

The sun shone low on the railway line
   And over the bricks and stacks,
And in at the upstairs windows
   Of the Dawley houses' backs,
When we saw the ghost of Captain Webb,
   Webb in a water sheeting,
Come dripping along in a bathing dress
   To the Saturday evening meeting.
       Dripping along –
       Dripping along –
       To the Congregational Hall;
Dripping and still he rose over the sill and faded away in a wall.

*'The Institute was radiant with gas.' Ch. XIX, *Boyhood*. A novel in verse by Rev. E. E. Bradford, D.D.

There wasn't a man in Oakengates
    That hadn't got hold of the tale,
And over the valley in Ironbridge,
    And round by Coalbrookdale,
How Captain Webb the Dawley man,
    Captain Webb from Dawley,
Rose rigid and dead from the old canal
    That carries the bricks to Lawley.
        Rigid and dead –
        Rigid and dead –
        To the Saturday congregation,
Paying a call at Dawley Bank on his way to his destination.

Upper Lambourne

Up the ash-tree climbs the ivy,
    Up the ivy climbs the sun,
With a twenty-thousand pattering
    Has a valley breeze begun,
Feathery ash, neglected elder,
    Shift the shade and make it run –

Shift the shade toward the nettles,
    And the nettles set it free
To streak the stained Carrara headstone
    Where, in nineteen-twenty-three,
He who trained a hundred winners
    Paid the Final Entrance Fee.

Leathery limbs of Upper Lambourne,
    Leathery skin from sun and wind,
Leathery breeches, spreading stables,
    Shining saddles left behind –
To the down the string of horses
    Moving out of sight and mind.

Feathery ash in leathery Lambourne
    Waves above the sarsen stone,
And Edwardian plantations
    So coniferously moan
As to make the swelling downland,
    Far-surrounding, seem their own.

Pot Pourri from a Surrey Garden

Miles of pram in the wind and Pam in the gorse track,
   Coco-nut smell of the broom, and a packet of Weights
Press'd in the sand. The thud of a hoof on a horse-track –
        A horse-riding horse for a horse-track –
        Conifer county of Surrey approached
   Through remarkable wrought-iron gates.

Over your boundary now, I wash my face in a bird-bath,
   Then which path shall I take? that over there by the pram?
Down by the pond! or – yes, I will take the slippery third path,
        Trodden away with gym shoes,
        Beautiful fir-dry alley that leads
   To the bountiful body of Pam.

Pam, I adore you, Pam, you great big mountainous sports girl,
   Whizzing them over the net, full of the strength of five:
That old Malvernian brother, you zephyr and khaki shorts girl,
        Although he's playing for Woking,
        Can't stand up
   To your wonderful backhand drive.

See the strength of her arm, as firm and hairy as Hendren's;
   See the size of her thighs, the pout of her lips as, cross,
And full of a pent-up strength, she swipes at the rhododendrons,
        Lucky the rhododendrons,
        And flings her arrogant love-lock
   Back with a petulant toss.

Over the redolent pinewoods, in at the bathroom casement,
  One fine Saturday, Windlesham bells shall call:
Up the Butterfield aisle rich with Gothic enlacement,
      Licensed now for embracement,
      Pam and I, as the organ
  Thunders over you all.

Trebetherick

We used to picnic where the thrift
    Grew deep and tufted to the edge;
We saw the yellow foam-flakes drift
    In trembling sponges on the ledge
Below us, till the wind would lift
    Them up the cliff and o'er the hedge.
Sand in the sandwiches, wasps in the tea,
Sun on our bathing-dresses heavy with the wet,
Squelch of the bladder-wrack waiting for the sea,
Fleas round the tamarisk, an early cigarette.

From where the coastguard houses stood
    One used to see, below the hill,
The lichened branches of a wood
    In summer silver-cool and still;
And there the Shade of Evil could
    Stretch out at us from Shilla Mill.
Thick with sloe and blackberry, uneven in the light,
Lonely ran the hedge, the heavy meadow was remote,
The oldest part of Cornwall was the wood as black as night,
And the pheasant and the rabbit lay torn open at the throat.

But when a storm was at its height,
    And feathery slate was black in rain,
And tamarisks were hung with light
    And golden sand was brown again,
Spring tide and blizzard would unite
    And sea came flooding up the lane.
Waves full of treasure then were roaring up the beach,
Ropes round our mackintoshes, waders warm and dry,
We waited for the wreckage to come swirling into reach,
Ralph, Vasey, Alastair, Biddy, John and I.

Then roller into roller curled
  And thundered down the rocky bay,
And we were in a water-world
  Of rain and blizzard, sea and spray,
And one against the other hurled
  We struggled round to Greenaway.
Blessèd be St Enodoc, blessèd be the wave,
Blessèd be the springy turf, we pray, pray to thee,
Ask for our children all the happy days you gave
To Ralph, Vasey, Alastair, Biddy, John and me.

Oxford: Sudden Illness at the Bus-stop

At the time of evening when cars run sweetly,
  Syringas blossom by Oxford gates.
In her evening velvet with a rose pinned neatly
  By the distant bus-stop a don's wife waits.

From that wide bedroom with its two branched lighting
  Over her looking-glass, up or down,
When sugar was short and the world was fighting
  She first appeared in that velvet gown.

What forks since then have been slammed in places?
  What peas turned out from how many a tin?
From plate-glass windows how many faces
  Have watched professors come hobbling in?

Too much, too many! so fetch the doctor,
  This dress has grown such a heavier load
Since Jack was only a Junior Proctor,
  And rents were lower in Rawlinson Road.

Group Life: Letchworth

Tell me Pippididdledum,
  Tell me how the children are.
Working each for weal of all
  After what you said.
Barry's on the common far
  Pedalling the Kiddie Kar.
Ann has had a laxative
  And Alured is dead.
Sympathy is stencilling
  Her decorative leatherwork,
Wilfred's learned a folk-tune for
  The Morris Dancers' band.
I have my ex-Service man and
  Mamie's done a lino-cut.
And Charlie's in the *kinderbank*
  A-kicking up the sand.
Wittle-tittle, wittle-tittle
  Toodle-oodle ducky birds,
What a lot my dicky chicky
  Tiny tots have done.
Wouldn't it be jolly now,
  To take our Aertex panters off
And have a jolly tumble in
  The jolly, jolly sun?

Sir John Piers

OH! BOLD BAD BARONET
YOU NEED NO CORONET
YOU SIGN YOUR WARRANT WITH
A BLOODY HAND.

Introduction

'In 1807, Sir John Piers, the last of the name who resided in Tristernagh, and who was a gambler, duellist, and spendthrift, was a schoolfellow of the patriot, Lord Cloncurry. Shortly after the marriage of that nobleman, Piers, who shared his hospitality, and even received pecuniary aid from him, made a diabolical wager to ruin for life the happiness of the wedded pair. Mr W. J. Fitzpatrick, the able biographer of Lord Cloncurry, says: "... A more unlikely person than Lady Cloncurry to prove unfaithful to him she had vowed to love, honour and obey, did not, perhaps, exist in Christendom. Can it be believed that such was the character which Sir John Piers resolved by every art of hell to wither and destroy? A bet, or agreement, as we have heard, was entered into between the monster and some kindred spirit, that in the event of the utter and complete ruin of Lord and Lady Cloncurry's happiness, a sum of money would be placed to the credit of his (Piers') account in a certain Dublin Bank. In case of failure, the operation was, of course, to be reversed ..."

'On the 19th of February, 1807, the celebrated trial, Cloncurry *v.* Piers, for crim. con., commenced in the Court of King's Bench before Lord Chief Justice Downes. Damages were laid at £100,000. The case created great interest and resulted in a verdict for the plaintiff, £20,000 and costs. John Philpot Curran and Charles Kendal Bushe were the leading Counsel for Lord Cloncurry, and their speeches were what might be expected from such gifted advocates. Those who would wish to read the speeches should consult *Curran and His Contemporaries*, by Charles Philips. Piers put in no appearance at the trial. Haunted by the near approach of retribution, he packed his portmanteau and fled to the Isle of Man. By this proceeding his recognizances became, of course, forfeited to the Crown. After a time the strong arm of the law secured him; he gave what he could reluctantly enough, and his bond for the remainder. Assailed on all sides by creditors, Sir John Piers had a cottage built at Tristernagh, surrounded by a high wall, to protect himself from the minions of justice; but ruin and misfortune overtook him; his estates were sold out in the Encumbered Estates Court.' (*Annals of Westmeath, Ancient and Modern,* by James Woods.)

I.   The Fête Champêtre

Oh, gay lapped the waves on the shores of Lough Ennel
And sweet smelt the breeze 'mid the garlic and fennel,
But sweeter and gayer than either of these
Were the songs of the birds in Lord Belvedere's trees.

The light skiff is push'd from the weed-waving shore,
The rowlocks creak evenly under the oar,
And a boatload of beauty darts over the tide,
The Baron Cloncurry and also his bride.

Lord Belvedere sits like a priest in the prow,
'Tis the Lady Mount Cashel sits next to him now.
And both the de Blacquieres to balance the boat,
Was so much nobility ever afloat?

The party's arranged on the opposite shore,
Lord Clonmore is present and one or two more,
But why has the Lady Cloncurry such fears?
Oh, one of the guests will be Baronet Piers.

The grotto is reached and the parties alight,
The feast is spread out, and begob! what a sight,
Pagodas of jelly in bowls of champagne,
And a tower of blancmange from the Baron Kilmaine.

In the shell-covered shelter the grotto affords
The meats and the pies are arranged on the boards,
The nobility laugh and are free from all worry
Excepting the bride of the Baron Cloncurry.

But his lordship is gayer than ever before,
He laughs like the ripples that lap the lake shore,
Nor thinks that his bride has the slightest of fears
Lest one of the guests be the Baronet Piers.

A curricle rolling along on the grass,
The servants make way to allow it to pass,
A high-stepping grey and the wheels flashing yellow
And Sir John in the seat, what a capital fellow!

Huzza for Sir John! and huzza for the fête,
For without his assistance no fête is complete;
Oh, gay is the garland the ladies will wreathe
For the handsomest blade in the County Westmeath.

The harness is off with a jingle of steel,
The grey in the grass crops an emerald meal,
Sir John saunters up with a smile and a bow
And the Lady Cloncurry is next to him now.

Her eyes on the landscape, she don't seem to hear
The passing remark he designs for her ear,
For smooth as a phantom and proud as a stork
The Lady Cloncurry continues her walk.

II.   The Attempt

I love your brown curls, | black in rain, my colleen,
   I love your grey eyes, | by this verdant shore
Two Derravaraghs | to plunge into and drown me,
   Hold not those lakes of | light so near me more.

My hand lies yellow | and hairy in your pink hand,
   Fragilis rubra | of the bramble flower,
Yet soft and thornless, | cool and as caressing
   As grasses bending | heavy with a shower.

See how the clouds twist | over in the twilight,
   See how the gale is | ruffling up the lake;
Lie still for ever | on this little peninsula,
   Heart beat and heart beat | steady till we wake.

Hear how the beech trees | roar above Glencara,
   See how the fungus | circles in the shade,
Roar trees and moan, you | gliding royal daughters,
   Circle us with poison, | we are not afraid.

Gothic on Gothic | my abbey soars around me,
   I've walks and avenues | emerald from rain,
Plentiful timber | in a lake reflected,
   And creamy meadowsweet | scenting my demesne.

Press to your cheeks | my hand so hot and wasted,
   Smooth with my fingers | the freckles of your frown,
Take you my abbey, | it is yours for always,
   I am so full of | love that I shall drown.

I lie by the lake water
And you, Cloncurry, not near,
I live in a girl's answer,
You, in a bawd's fear.

III.   The Exile

On Mannin's rough coast-line the twilight descending
  With its last dying rays on thy height, O Snaefell!
A refuge of dark to the Island is lending
  And to yon *cottage ornée* that lies in the dell.

Its helpless inhabitant dare not appear in
  The rain-weathered streets of adjacent Rumsaa,
But he sees in his dreams the green island of Erin
  And he sits in an orat'ry most of the day.

Yet sometimes, at night, when the waves in commotion
  Are tumbling about round the long point of Ayr,
He strides through the tamarisks down to the ocean
  Beyond the lush curraghs of sylvan Lezayre.

Alone with his thoughts when the wild waves are beating
  He walks round to Jurby along the wet sand,
And there, where the moon shows the waves are retreating,
  He too would retreat to his own native land.

IV.   The Return

My speculated avenues are wasted,
  The artificial lake is choked and dry,
My old delight by other lips is tasted,
  Now I can only build my walls and die.

I'll nail the southern wall with Irish peaches,
  Portloman cuttings warmed in silver suns,
And eastwards to Lough Iron's reedy reaches
  I'll build against the vista and the duns.

To westward where the avenue approaches
  Since they have felled the trees of my demesne,
And since I'll not be visited by coaches,
  I'll build a mighty wall against the rain.

And from the North, lest you, Malone, should spy me,
  You, Sunderlin of Baronstown, the peer,
I'll fill your eye with all the stone that's by me
  And live four-square protected in my fear.

Blue dragonflies dart on and do not settle,
  Live things stay not; although my walls are high,
They keep not out the knapweed and the nettle,
  Stone are my coffin walls, waiting till I die.

V. Tristernagh Today

In the ivy dusty is the old lock rusty
    That opens rasping on the place of graves,
'Tis no home for mortals behind those portals
    Where the shining dock grows and the nettle waves.
Of the walls so ferny, near Tristernagh churchyard,
    Often the learned historians write,
And the Abbey splendificent, most magnificent,
    Ribbed and springing in ancient night.

Kyrie elëeison! blessed St Bison!
    Holy Piran! Veronica's Veil!
SS Columb, Colman and St Attracta,
    Likewise St Hector, please aid my tale!
Holy Virgin! What's that emergin'?
    I daren't go down in the place of graves,
Head of a dragonfly, twenty times magnified,
    Creeping diagonal, out of the caves!

Dockleaves lapping it, maidenhair flapping it,
    Blue veins mapping it, skin of the moon,
Suck of the bog in it, cold of the frog in it,
    Keep it away from me, shrouded cocoon.
The worms are moving this soft and smooth thing
    And I'm the creature for foolish fears,
There's not a feature that's super nature
    'Tis only rational, 'tis

SIR
JOHN
PIERS.

Myfanwy

Kind o'er the *kinderbank* leans my Myfanwy,
　White o'er the play-pen the sheen of her dress,
Fresh from the bathroom and soft in the nursery
　Soap-scented fingers I long to caress.

Were you a prefect and head of your dormit'ry?
　Were you a hockey girl, tennis or gym?
Who was your favourite? Who had a crush on you?
　Which were the baths where they taught you to swim?

Smooth down the Avenue glitters the bicycle,
　Black-stockinged legs under navy-blue serge,
Home and Colonial, Star, International,
　Balancing bicycle leant on the verge.

Trace me your wheel-tracks, you fortunate bicycle,
　Out of the shopping and into the dark,
Back down the Avenue, back to the pottingshed,
　Back to the house on the fringe of the park.

Golden the light on the locks of Myfanwy,
　Golden the light on the book on her knee,
Finger-marked pages of Rackham's Hans Andersen,
　Time for the children to come down to tea.

Oh! Fuller's angel-cake, Robertson's marmalade,
　Liberty lampshade, come, shine on us all,
My! what a spread for the friends of Myfanwy
　Some in the alcove and some in the hall.

Then what sardines in the half-lighted passages!
Locking of fingers in long hide-and-seek.
You will protect me, my silken Myfanwy,
    Ringleader, tom-boy, and chum to the weak.

In Westminster Abbey

Let me take this other glove off
　As the *vox humana* swells,
And the beauteous fields of Eden
　Bask beneath the Abbey bells.
Here, where England's statesmen lie,
Listen to a lady's cry.

Gracious Lord, oh bomb the Germans.
　Spare their women for Thy Sake,
And if that is not too easy
　We will pardon Thy Mistake.
But, gracious Lord, whate'er shall be,
Don't let anyone bomb me.

Keep our Empire undismembered
　Guide our Forces by Thy Hand,
Gallant blacks from far Jamaica,
　Honduras and Togoland;
Protect them Lord in all their fights,
And, even more, protect the whites.

Think of what our Nation stands for,
　Books from Boots' and country lanes,
Free speech, free passes, class distinction,
　Democracy and proper drains.
Lord, put beneath Thy special care
One-eighty-nine Cadogan Square.

Although dear Lord I am a sinner,
　I have done no major crime;
Now I'll come to Evening Service
　Whensoever I have the time.

So, Lord, reserve for me a crown,
And do not let my shares go down.

I will labour for Thy Kingdom,
    Help our lads to win the war,
Send white feathers to the cowards
    Join the Women's Army Corps,
Then wash the Steps around Thy Throne
In the Eternal Safety Zone.

Now I feel a little better,
    What a treat to hear Thy Word,
Where the bones of leading statesmen
    Have so often been interr'd.
And now, dear Lord, I cannot wait
Because I have a luncheon date.

Senex

Oh would I could subdue the flesh
   Which sadly troubles me!
And then perhaps could view the flesh
As though I never knew the flesh
   And merry misery.

To see the golden hiking girl
   With wind about her hair,
The tennis-playing, biking girl,
The wholly-to-my-liking girl,
   To see and not to care.

At sundown on my tricycle
   I tour the Borough's edge,
And icy as an icicle
See bicycle by bicycle
   Stacked waiting in the hedge.

Get down from me! I thunder there,
   You spaniels! Shut your jaws!
Your teeth are stuffed with underwear,
Suspenders torn asunder there
   And buttocks in your paws!

Oh whip the dogs away my Lord,
   They make me ill with lust.
Bend bare knees down to pray, my Lord,
Teach sulky lips to say, my Lord,
   That flaxen hair is dust.

On a Portrait of a Deaf Man

The kind old face, the egg-shaped head,
　　The tie, discreetly loud,
The loosely fitting shooting clothes,
　　A closely fitting shroud.

He liked old City dining-rooms,
　　Potatoes in their skin,
But now his mouth is wide to let
　　The London clay come in.

He took me on long silent walks
　　In country lanes when young,
He knew the name of ev'ry bird
　　But not the song it sung.

And when he could not hear me speak
　　He smiled and looked so wise
That now I do not like to think
　　Of maggots in his eyes.

He liked the rain-washed Cornish air
　　And smell of ploughed-up soil,
He liked a landscape big and bare
　　And painted it in oil.

But least of all he liked that place
　　Which hangs on Highgate Hill
Of soaked Carrara-covered earth
　　For Londoners to fill.

He would have liked to say good-bye,
    Shake hands with many friends,
In Highgate now his finger-bones
    Stick through his finger-ends.

You, God, who treat him thus and thus,
    Say 'Save his soul and pray.'
You ask me to believe You and
    I only see decay.

Henley-on-Thames

I see the winding water make
A short and then a shorter lake
    As here stand I,
    And house-boat high
Survey the Upper Thames.
  By sun the mud is amber-dyed
  In ripples slow and flat and wide,
   That flap against the house-boat side
And flop away in gems.

In mud and elder-scented shade
A reach away the breach is made
    By dive and shout
    That circles out
To Henley tower and town;
  And 'Boats for Hire' the rafters ring,
  And pink on white the roses cling,
  And red the bright geraniums swing
In baskets dangling down.

When shall I see the Thames again?
The prow-promoted gems again,
    As beefy ATS
    Without their hats
Come shooting through the bridge?
  And 'cheerioh' and 'cheeri-bye'
  Across the waste of waters die,
  And low the mists of evening lie
And lightly skims the midge.

Parliament Hill Fields

Rumbling under blackened girders, Midland, bound for
Cricklewood,
Puffed its sulphur to the sunset where that Land of Laundries stood.
Rumble under, thunder over, train and tram alternate go,
Shake the floor and smudge the ledger, Charrington, Sells, Dale and
Co.,
Nuts and nuggets in the window, trucks along the lines below.

When the Bon Marché was shuttered, when the feet were hot and
tired,
Outside Charrington's we waited, by the 'STOP HERE IF
REQUIRED',
Launched aboard the shopping basket, sat precipitately down,
Rocked past Zwanziger the baker's, and the terrace blackish brown,
And the curious Anglo-Norman parish church of Kentish Town.

Till the tram went over thirty, sighting terminus again,
Past municipal lawn tennis and the bobble-hanging plane;
Soft the light suburban evening caught our ashlar-speckled spire,
Eighteen-sixty Early English, as the mighty elms retire
Either side of Brookfield Mansions flashing fine French-window fire.

Oh the after-tram-ride quiet, when we heard a mile beyond,
Silver music from the bandstand, barking dogs by Highgate Pond;
Up the hill where stucco houses in Virginia creeper drown –
And my childish wave of pity, seeing children carrying down
Sheaves of drooping dandelions to the courts of Kentish Town.

A Subaltern's Love-song

Miss J. Hunter Dunn, Miss J. Hunter Dunn,
Furnish'd and burnish'd by Aldershot sun,
What strenuous singles we played after tea,
We in the tournament – you against me!

Love-thirty, love-forty, oh! weakness of joy,
The speed of a swallow, the grace of a boy,
With carefullest carelessness, gaily you won,
I am weak from your loveliness, Joan Hunter Dunn.

Miss Joan Hunter Dunn, Miss Joan Hunter Dunn,
How mad I am, sad I am, glad that you won.
The warm-handled racket is back in its press,
But my shock-headed victor, she loves me no less.

Her father's euonymus shines as we walk,
And swing past the summer-house, buried in talk,
And cool the verandah that welcomes us in
To the six-o'clock news and a lime-juice and gin.

The scent of the conifers, sound of the bath,
The view from my bedroom of moss-dappled path,
As I struggle with double-end evening tie,
For we dance at the Golf Club, my victor and I.

On the floor of her bedroom lie blazer and shorts
And the cream-coloured walls are be-trophied with sports,
And westering, questioning settles the sun
On your low-leaded window, Miss Joan Hunter Dunn.

The Hillman is waiting, the light's in the hall,
The pictures of Egypt are bright on the wall,
My sweet, I am standing beside the oak stair
And there on the landing's the light on your hair.

By roads 'not adopted', by woodlanded ways,
She drove to the club in the late summer haze,
Into nine-o'clock Camberley, heavy with bells
And mushroomy, pine-woody, evergreen smells.

Miss Joan Hunter Dunn, Miss Joan Hunter Dunn,
I can hear from the car-park the dance has begun.
Oh! full Surrey twilight! importunate band!
Oh! strongly adorable tennis-girl's hand!

Around us are Rovers and Austins afar,
Above us, the intimate roof of the car,
And here on my right is the girl of my choice,
With the tilt of her nose and the chime of her voice,

And the scent of her wrap, and the words never said,
And the ominous, ominous dancing ahead.
We sat in the car-park till twenty to one
And now I'm engaged to Miss Joan Hunter Dunn.

Bristol

Green upon the flooded Avon shone the after-storm-wet-sky
Quick the struggling withy branches let the leaves of autumn fly
And a star shone over Bristol, wonderfully far and high.

Ringers in an oil-lit belfry – Bitton? Kelston? who shall say? –
Smoothly practising a plain course, caverned out the dying day
As their melancholy music flooded up and ebbed away.

Then all Somerset was round me and I saw the clippers ride,
High above the moonlit houses, triple-masted on the tide,
By the tall embattled church-towers of the Bristol waterside.

And an undersong to branches dripping into pools and wells
Out of multitudes of elm trees over leagues of hills and dells
Was the mathematic pattern of a plain course on the bells.*

*1	2	2	4	4	5	5	3	3	1	1
2	1	4	2	5	4	3	5	1	3	2
3	4	1	5	2	3	4	1	5	2	3
4	3	5	1	3	2	1	4	2	5	4
5	5	3	3	1	1	2	2	4	4	5

Ireland with Emily

Bells are booming down the bohreens,
  White the mist along the grass.
Now the Julias, Maeves and Maureens
  Move between the fields to Mass.
Twisted trees of small green apple
Guard the decent whitewashed chapel,
Gilded gates and doorway grained
Pointed windows richly stained
  With many-coloured Munich glass.

See the black-shawled congregations
  On the broidered vestment gaze
Murmur past the painted stations
  As Thy Sacred Heart displays
Lush Kildare of scented meadows,
Roscommon, thin in ash-tree shadows,
And Westmeath the lake-reflected,
Spreading Leix the hill-protected,
  Kneeling all in silver haze?

In yews and woodbine, walls and guelder,
  Nettle-deep the faithful rest,
Winding leagues of flowering elder,
  Sycamore with ivy dressed,
Ruins in demesnes deserted,
Bog-surrounded bramble-skirted –
Townlands rich or townlands mean as
These, oh, counties of them screen us
  In the Kingdom of the West.

Stony seaboard, far and foreign,
   Stony hills poured over space,
Stony outcrop of the Burren,
   Stones in every fertile place,
Little fields with boulders dotted,
Grey-stone shoulders saffron-spotted,
Stone-walled cabins thatched with reeds,
Where a Stone Age people breeds
   The last of Europe's stone age race.

Has it held, the warm June weather?
   Draining shallow sea-pools dry,
When we bicycled together
   Down the bohreens fuchsia-high.
Till there rose, abrupt and lonely,
A ruined abbey, chancel only,
Lichen-crusted, time-befriended,
Soared the arches, splayed and splendid,
   Romanesque against the sky.

There in pinnacled protection,
   One extinguished family waits
A Church of Ireland resurrection
   By the broken, rusty gates.
Sheepswool, straw and droppings cover,
Graves of spinster, rake and lover,
Whose fantastic mausoleum
Sings its own seablown Te Deum,
   In and out the slipping slates.

In a Bath Teashop

'Let us not speak, for the love we bear one another –
    Let us hold hands and look.'
She, such a very ordinary little woman;
    He, such a thumping crook;
But both, for a moment, little lower than the angels
    In the teashop's ingle-nook.

Before the Anaesthetic,
or
A Real Fright

Intolerably sad, profound
St Giles's bells are ringing round,
They bring the slanting summer rain
To tap the chestnut boughs again
Whose shadowy cave of rainy leaves
The gusty belfry-song receives.
Intolerably sad and true,
Victorian red and jewel* blue,
The mellow bells are ringing round
And charge the evening light with sound,
And I look motionless from bed
On heavy trees and purple red
And hear the midland bricks and tiles
Throw back the bells of stone St Giles,
Bells, ancient now as castle walls,
Now hard and new as pitchpine stalls,
Now full with help from ages past,
Now dull with death and hell at last.
Swing up! and give me hope of life,
Swing down! and plunge the surgeon's knife.
I, breathing for a moment, see
Death wing himself away from me
And think, as on this bed I lie,
Is it extinction when I die?
I move my limbs and use my sight;
Not yet, thank God, not yet the Night.
Oh better far those echoing hells

*Adjective from Rumer Godden.

Half-threaten'd in the pealing bells
Than that this 'I' should cease to be –
Come quickly, Lord, come quick to me.
St Giles's bells are asking now
'And hast thou known the Lord, hast thou?'
St Giles's bells, they richly ring
'And was that Lord our Christ the King?'
St Giles's bells they hear me call
I never knew the Lord at all.
Oh not in me your Saviour dwells
You ancient, rich St Giles's bells.
Illuminated missals – spires –
Wide screens and decorated quires –
All these I loved, and on my knees
I thanked myself for knowing these
And watched the morning sunlight pass
Through richly stained Victorian glass
And in the colour-shafted air
I, kneeling, thought the Lord was there.
Now, lying in the gathering mist
I know that Lord did not exist;
Now, lest this 'I' should cease to be,
Come, real Lord, come quick to me.
With every gust the chestnut sighs,
With every breath, a mortal dies;
The man who smiled alone, alone,
And went his journey on his own
With 'Will you give my wife this letter,
In case, of course, I don't get better?'
Waits for his coffin lid to close
On waxen head and yellow toes.
Almighty Saviour, had I Faith
There'd be no fight with kindly Death.
Intolerably long and deep
St Giles's bells swing on in sleep:
'But still you go from here alone'
Say all the bells about the Throne.

Youth and Age on Beaulieu River, Hants

Early sun on Beaulieu water
　　Lights the undersides of oaks,
Clumps of leaves it floods and blanches,
All transparent glow the branches
　　Which the double sunlight soaks;
To her craft on Beaulieu water
Clemency the General's daughter
　　Pulls across with even strokes.

Schoolboy-sure she is this morning;
　　Soon her sharpie's rigg'd and free.
Cool beneath a garden awning
　　Mrs Fairclough, sipping tea
And raising large long-distance glasses
As the little sharpie passes,
　　Sighs our sailor girl to see:

Tulip figure, so appealing,
　　Oval face, so serious-eyed,
Tree-roots pass'd and muddy beaches.
On to huge and lake-like reaches,
　　Soft and sun-warm, see her glide –
Slacks the slim young limbs revealing,
Sun-brown arm the tiller feeling –
　　With the wind and with the tide.

Evening light will bring the water,
　　Day-long sun will burst the bud,
Clemency, the General's daughter,
　　Will return upon the flood.
But the older woman only
Knows the ebb-tide leaves her lonely
　　With the shining fields of mud.

Lines from Sunday Afternoon Service in St Enodoc Church, Cornwall

... Where deep cliffs loom enormous, where cascade
Mesembryanthemum and stone-crop down,
Where the gull looks no larger than a lark
Hung midway twixt the cliff-top and the sand,
Sun-shadowed valleys roll along the sea.
Forced by the backwash, see the nearest wave
Rise to a wall of huge, translucent green
And crumble into spray along the top
Blown seaward by the land-breeze. Now she breaks
And in an arch of thunder plunges down
To burst and tumble, foam on top of foam,
Criss-crossing, baffled, sucked and shot again,
A waterfall of whiteness, down a rock,
Without a source but roller's furthest reach:
And tufts of sea-pink, high and dry for years,
Are flooded out of ledges, boulders seem
No bigger than a pebble washed about
In this tremendous tide. ...

Indoor Games near Newbury

In among the silver birches winding ways of tarmac wander
  And the signs to Bussock Bottom, Tussock Wood and Windy
                                    Brake,
Gabled lodges, tile-hung churches, catch the lights of our Lagonda
  As we drive to Wendy's party, lemon curd and Christmas cake.
      Rich the makes of motor whirring,
      Past the pine-plantation purring
         Come up, Hupmobile, Delage!
      Short the way your chauffeurs travel,
      Crunching over private gravel
         Each from out his warm garáge.

Oh but Wendy, when the carpet yielded to my indoor pumps
      There you stood, your gold hair streaming,
      Handsome in the hall-light gleaming
There you looked and there you led me off into the game of clumps
      Then the new Victrola playing
      And your funny uncle saying
'Choose your partners for a fox-trot! Dance until its *tea* o'clock!
  'Come on, young 'uns, foot it featly!'
  Was it chance that paired us neatly,
  I, who loved you so completely,
You, who pressed me closely to you, hard against your party frock?

'Meet me when you've finished eating!' So we met and no one found
                       us.
  Oh that dark and furry cupboard while the rest played hide and
                       seek!
Holding hands our two hearts beating in the bedroom silence round
                       us,
  Holding hands and hardly hearing sudden footstep, thud and
                       shriek.

Love that lay too deep for kissing –
'Where *is* Wendy? Wendy's missing!'
Love so pure it *had* to end,
Love so strong that I was frighten'd
When you gripped my fingers tight and
Hugging, whispered 'I'm your friend.'

Good-bye Wendy! Send the fairies, pinewood elf and larch tree
gnome,
Spingle-spangled stars are peeping
At the lush Lagonda creeping
Down the winding ways of tarmac to the leaded lights of home.
There, among the silver birches,
All the bells of all the churches
Sounded in the bath-waste running out into the frosty air.
Wendy speeded my undressing,
Wendy is the sheet's caressing
Wendy bending gives a blessing,
Holds me as I drift to dreamland, safe inside my slumberwear.

St Saviour's, Aberdeen Park, Highbury, London, N.

With oh such peculiar branching and over-reaching of wire
    Trolley-bus standards pick their threads from the London sky
Diminishing up the perspective, Highbury-bound retire
    Threads and buses and standards with plane trees volleying by
And, more peculiar still, that ever-increasing spire
    Bulges over the housetops, polychromatic and high.

Stop the trolley-bus, stop! And here, where the roads unite
    Of weariest worn-out London – no cigarettes, no beer,
No repairs undertaken, nothing in stock – alight;
    For over the waste of willow-herb, look at her, sailing clear,
A great Victorian church, tall, unbroken and bright
    In a sun that's setting in Willesden and saturating us here.

These were the streets my parents knew when they loved and won –
    The brougham that crunched the gravel, the laurel-girt paths that
                                      wind,
Geranium-beds for the lawn, Venetian blinds for the sun,
    A separate tradesman's entrance, straw in the mews behind,
Just in the four-mile radius where hackney carriages run,
    Solid Italianate houses for the solid commercial mind.

These were the streets they knew; and I, by descent, belong
    To these tall neglected houses divided into flats.
Only the church remains, where carriages used to throng
    And my mother stepped out in flounces and my father stepped out
                                      in spats
To shadowy stained-glass matins or gas-lit evensong
    And back in a country quiet with doffing of chimney hats.

Great red church of my parents, cruciform crossing they knew –
    Over these same encaustics they and their parents trod
Bound through a red-brick transept for a once familiar pew
    Where the organ set them singing and the sermon let them nod
And up this coloured brickwork the same long shadows grew
    As these in the stencilled chancel where I kneel in the presence of
        God.

Wonder beyond Time's wonders, that Bread so white and small
    Veiled in golden curtains, too mighty for men to see,
Is the Power which sends the shadows up this polychrome wall,
    Is God who created the present, the chain-smoking millions and
        me;
Beyond the throb of the engines is the throbbing heart of all –
    Christ, at this Highbury altar, I offer myself to Thee.

Beside the Seaside

Green Shutters, shut your shutters! Windyridge,
Let winds unnoticed whistle round your hill!
High Dormers, draw your curtains! Slam the door,
And pack the family in the Morris eight.
Lock up the garage. Put her in reverse,
Back out with care, now, forward, off – away!
The richer people living farther out
O'ertake us in their Rovers. We, in turn,
Pass poorer families hurrying on foot
Towards the station. Very soon the town
Will echo to the groan of empty trams
And sweetshops advertise Ice Cream in vain.
Solihull, Headingley and Golders Green.
Preston and Swindon, Manchester and Leeds,
Braintree and Bocking, hear the sea! the sea!
The smack of breakers upon windy rocks,
Spray blowing backwards from their curling walls
Of green translucent water. England leaves
Her centre for her tide-line. Father's toes,
Though now encased in coloured socks and shoes
And pressing the accelerator hard,
Ache for the feel of sand and little shrimps
To tickle in between them. Mother vows
To be more patient with the family:
Just for its sake she will be young again.
And, at that moment, Jennifer is sick
(Over-excitement must have brought it on,
The hurried breakfast and the early start)
And Michael's rather pale, and as for Anne . . .
'Please stop a moment, Hubert, anywhere.'
   So evening sunlight shows us Sandy Cove
The same as last year and the year before.

Still on the brick front of the Baptist Church
SIX-THIRTY. PREACHER: – *Mr Pentecost* –
All visitors are welcomed. Still the quartz
Glitters along the tops of garden walls.
Those macrocarpa still survive the gales
They must have had last winter. Still the shops
Remain unaltered on the Esplanade –
The Circulating Library, the Stores,
Jill's Pantry, Cynthia's Ditty Box (Antiques),
Trecarrow (Maps and Souvenirs and Guides).
Still on the terrace of the big hotel
Pale pink hydrangeas turn a rusty brown
Where sea winds catch them, and yet do not die.
The bumpy lane between the tamarisks,
The escallonia hedge, and still it's there –
Our lodging-house, ten minutes from the shore.
Still unprepared to make a picnic lunch
Except by notice on the previous day.
Still nowhere for the children when it's wet
Except that smelly, overcrowded lounge.
And still no garage for the motor-car.
Still on the bedroom wall, the list of rules:
Don't waste the water. It is pumped by hand.
Don't throw old blades into the W.C.
Don't keep the bathroom long and don't be late
For meals and don't hang swim-suits out on sills
(A line has been provided at the back).
Don't empty children's sand-shoes in the hall.
Don't this, Don't that. Ah, still the same, the same
As it was last year and the year before –
But rather more expensive, now, of course.
'Anne, Jennifer and Michael – run along
Down to the sands and find yourselves some friends
While Dad and I unpack.' The sea! the sea!
   On a secluded corner of the beach
A game of rounders has been organized
By Mr Pedder, schoolmaster and friend
Of boys and girls – particularly girls.

And here it was the tragedy began,
That life-long tragedy to Jennifer
Which ate into her soul and made her take
To secretarial work in later life
In a department of the Board of Trade.
See boys and girls assembled for the game.
Reflected in the rock pools, freckled legs
Hop, skip and jump in coltish ecstasy.
Ah! parted lips and little pearly teeth,
Wide eyes, snub noses, shorts, divided skirts!
And last year's queen of them was Jennifer.
The snubbiest, cheekiest, lissomest of all.
One smile from her sent Mr Pedder back
Contented to his lodgings. She could wave
Her little finger and the elder boys
Came at her bidding. Even tiny Ruth,
Old Lady D'Erncourt's grandchild, pet of all,
Would bring her shells as timid offerings.
So now with Anne and Michael see her stand,
Our Jennifer, our own, our last year's queen,
For this year's *début* fully confident.
'Get in your places.' Heard above the waves
Are Mr Pedder's organizing shouts.
'Come on. Look sharp. The tide is coming in!'
'He hasn't seen me yet,' thinks Jennifer.
'Line up your team behind you, Christabel!'
On the wet sea-sand waiting to be seen
She stands with Anne and Michael. Let him turn
And then he'll see me. Let him only turn.
Smack went the tennis ball. The bare feet ran.
And smack again. 'He's out! Well caught, Delphine!'
Shrieks, cartwheels, tumbling joyance of the waves.
Oh Mr Pedder, look! Oh here I am!
And there the three of them forlornly stood.
'You ask him, Jennifer.' 'No – Michael? – Anne?'
'I'd rather not.' 'Fains I.' 'It's up to you.'
'Oh, very well, then.' Timidly she goes,

Timid and proud, for the last time a child.
'Can *we* play, Mr Pedder?' But his eyes
Are out to where, among the tousled heads,
He sees the golden curls of Christabel.
'Can *we* play, Mr Pedder?' So he turns.
'*Who* have we here?' The jolly, jolly voice,
The same but not the same. '*Who* have we here?
The Rawlings children! Yes, of course, you may,
Join that side, children, under Christabel.'
No friendly wallop on the B.T.M.
No loving arm-squeeze and no special look.
Oh darting heart-burn, *under Christabel!*
So all those holidays the bitter truth
Sank into Jennifer. No longer queen,
She had outgrown her strength, as Mummy said,
And Mummy made her wear these spectacles.
Because of Mummy she had lost her looks.
Had lost her looks? Still she was Jennifer.
The sands were still the same, the rocks the same,
The seaweed-waving pools, the bathing-cove,
The outline of the cliffs, the times of tide.
And I'm the same, of course I'm always M E.
But all that August those terrific waves
Thundered defeat along the rocky coast,
And ginger-beery surf hissed 'Christabel!' ...

And all the time the waves, the waves, the waves
Chase, intersect and flatten on the sand
As they have done for centuries, as they will
For centuries to come, when not a soul
Is left to picnic on the blazing rocks,
When England is not England, when mankind
Has blown himself to pieces. Still the sea,
Consolingly disastrous, will return
While the strange starfish, hugely magnified,
Waits in the jewelled basin of a pool.

North Coast Recollections

No people on the golf-links, not a crack
Of well-swung driver from the fourteenth tee,
No sailing bounding ball across the turf
And lady's slipper of the fairway. Black
Rises Bray Hill and, Stepper-wards, the sun
Sends Bray Hill's phantom stretching to the church.
The lane, the links, the beach, the cliffs are bare
The neighbourhood is dressing for a dance
And lamps are being lit in bungalows.
  O! thymy time of evening: clover scent
And feathery tamarisk round the churchyard wall
And shrivelled sea-pinks and this foreshore pale
With silver sand and sharpened quartz and slate
And brittle twigs, bleached, salted and prepared
For kindling blue-flamed fires on winter nights.
  Here Petroc landed, here I stand today;
The same Atlantic surges roll for me
As rolled for Parson Hawker and for him,
And spent their gathering thunder on the rocks
Crashing with pebbly backwash, burst again
And strewed the nibbled fields along the cliffs.

  When low tides drain the estuary gold
Small intersecting breakers far away
Ripple about a bar of shifting sand
Where centuries ago were waving woods
Where centuries hence, there will be woods again.

  Within the bungalow of Mrs Hanks
Her daughter Phoebe now French-chalks the floor.
Norman and Gordon in their dancing pumps
Slide up and down, but can't make concrete smooth.

'My Sweet Hortense . . .'
Sings louder down the garden than the sea.
'A practice record, Phoebe. Mummykins,
Gordon and I will do the washing-up.'
'We picnic here; we scrounge and help ourselves,'
Says Mrs Hanks, and visitors will smile
To see them all turn to it. Boys and girls
Weed in the sterile garden, mostly sand
And dead tomato-plants and chicken-runs.
Today they cleaned the dulled Benares ware
(Dulled by the sea-mist), early made the beds,
And Phoebe twirled the icing round the cake
And Gordon tinkered with the gramophone
While into an immense enamel jug
Norman poured 'Eiffel Tower' for lemonade.
    O! healthy bodies, bursting into 'teens
And bursting out of last year's summer clothes,
Fluff barking and French windows banging to
Till the asbestos walling of the place
Shakes with the life it shelters, and with all
The preparations for this evening's dance.

    Now drains the colour from the convolvulus,
The windows of Trenain are flashing fire,
Black sways the tamarisk against the West,
And bathing things are taken in from sills.
One child still zig-zags homewards up the lane,
Cold on bare feet he feels the dew-wet sand.
Behind him, from a walk along the cliff,
Come pater and the mater and the dogs.

    Four macrocarpa hide the tennis club.
Two children of a chartered actuary
(Beaworthy, Trouncer, Heppelwhite and Co.),
Harold and Bonzo Trouncer are engaged
In semi-finals for the tournament.
'Love thirty!' Pang! across the evening air

Twangs Harold's racquet. Plung! the ball returns.
Experience at Budleigh Salterton
Keeps Bonzo steady at the net. 'Well done!'
'Love forty!' Captain Mycroft, midst applause,
Pronounces for the Trouncers, to be sure
He can't be certain Bonzo didn't reach
A shade across the net, but Demon Sex,
That tulip figure in white cotton dress,
Bare legs, wide eyes and so tip-tilted nose
Quite overset him. Harold serves again
And Mrs Pardon says it's getting cold,
Miss Myatt shivers, Lady Lambourn thinks
These English evenings are a little damp
And dreams herself again in fair Shanghai.
'Game . . . AND! and thank you!'; so the pair from Rock
(A neighbouring and less exclusive place)
Defeated, climb into their Morris Ten.
'The final is tomorrow! Well, good night!'
    He lay in wait, he lay in wait, he did,
John Lambourn, curly-headed; dewy grass
Dampened his flannels, but he still remained.
The sunset drained the colours black and gold,
From his all-glorious First Eleven scarf.
But still he waited by the twilit hedge.
Only his eyes blazed blue with early love,
Blue blazing in the darkness of the lane,
Blue blazer, less incalculably blue,
Dark scarf, white flannels, supple body still,
First love, first light, first life. A heartbeat noise!
His heart or little feet? A snap of twigs
Dry, dead and brown the under branches part
And Bonzo scrambles by their secret way.
First love so deep, John Lambourn cannot speak,
So deep, he feels a tightening in his throat,
So tender, he could brush away the sand
Dried up in patches on her freckled legs,
Could hold her gently till the stars went down,

And if she cut herself would staunch the wound,
Yes, even with this First Eleven scarf,
And hold it there for hours.
So happy, and so deep he loves the world,
Could worship God and rocks and stones and trees,
Be nicer to his mother, kill himself
If that would make him pure enough for her.
And so at last he manages to say
'You going to the Hanks's hop tonight?'
'Well, I'm not sure. Are you?' 'I think I may –
'It's pretty dud though – only lemonade.'

    Sir Gawain was a right and goodly knight
Nor ever wist he to uncurtis be.
So old, so lovely, and so very true!
Then Mrs Wilder shut the Walter Crane
And tied the tapes and tucked her youngest in
What time without amidst the lavender
At late last 'He' played Primula and Prue
With new-found liveliness, for bed was soon.
And in the garage, serious seventeen
Harvey, the eldest, hammered on, content,
Fixing a mizzen to his model boat.
'Coo-ee! Coo-ee!' across the lavender,
Across the mist of pale gypsophila
And lolling purple poppies, Mumsie called,
A splendid sunset lit the rocking-horse
And Morris pattern of the nursery walls.
'Coo-ee!' the slate-hung, goodly-builded house
And sunset-sodden garden fell to quiet.
'Prue! Primsie! Mumsie wants you. Sleepi-byes!'
Prue jumped the marigolds and hid herself,
Her sister scampered to the Wendy Hut
And Harvey, glancing at his Ingersoll,
Thought 'Damn! I must get ready for the dance.'

So on this after-storm-lit evening
To Jim the raindrops in the tamarisk,
The fuchsia bells, the sodden matchbox lid
That checked a tiny torrent in the lane
Were magnified and shining clear with life.
Then pealing out across the estuary
The Padstow bells rang up for practice-night
An undersong to birds and dripping shrubs.
The full Atlantic at September spring
Flooded a final tide-mark up the sand,
And ocean sank to silence under bells,
And the next breaker was a lesser one
Then lesser still. Atlantic, bells and birds
Were layer on interchanging layers of sound.

Harrow-on-the-Hill

When melancholy Autumn comes to Wembley
  And electric trains are lighted after tea
The poplars near the Stadium are trembly
  With their tap and tap and whispering to me,
    Like the sound of little breakers
    Spreading out along the surf-line
When the estuary's filling
    With the sea.

Then Harrow-on-the-Hill's a rocky island
  And Harrow churchyard full of sailors' graves
And the constant click and kissing of the trolley buses hissing
  Is the level to the Wealdstone turned to waves
    And the rumble of the railway
    Is the thunder of the rollers
As they gather up for plunging
    Into caves.

There's a storm cloud to the westward over Kenton,
  There's a line of harbour lights at Perivale,
Is it rounding rough Pentire in a flood of sunset fire
  The little fleet of trawlers under sail?
    Can those boats be only roof tops
    As they stream along the skyline
In a race for port and Padstow
    With the gale?

Christmas

The bells of waiting Advent ring,
   The Tortoise stove is lit again
And lamp-oil light across the night
   Has caught the streaks of winter rain
In many a stained-glass window sheen
From Crimson Lake to Hooker's Green.

The holly in the windy hedge
   And round the Manor House the yew
Will soon be stripped to deck the ledge,
   The altar, font and arch and pew,
So that the villagers can say
'The church looks nice' on Christmas Day.

Provincial public houses blaze
   And Corporation tramcars clang,
On lighted tenements I gaze
   Where paper decorations hang,
And bunting in the red Town Hall
Says 'Merry Christmas to you all.'

And London shops on Christmas Eve
   Are strung with silver bells and flowers
As hurrying clerks the City leave
   To pigeon-haunted classic towers,
And marbled clouds go scudding by
The many-steepled London sky.

And girls in slacks remember Dad,
   And oafish louts remember Mum,
And sleepless children's hearts are glad,
   And Christmas-morning bells say 'Come!'

Even to shining ones who dwell
Safe in the Dorchester Hotel.

And is it true? And is it true,
    This most tremendous tale of all,
Seen in a stained-glass window's hue,
    A Baby in an ox's stall?
The Maker of the stars and sea
Become a Child on earth for me?

And is it true? For if it is,
    No loving fingers tying strings
Around those tissued fripperies,
    The sweet and silly Christmas things,
Bath salts and inexpensive scent
And hideous tie so kindly meant,

No love that in a family dwells,
    No carolling in frosty air,
Nor all the steeple-shaking bells
    Can with this single Truth compare –
That God was Man in Palestine
And lives today in Bread and Wine.

The Licorice Fields at Pontefract

In the licorice fields at Pontefract
   My love and I did meet
And many a burdened licorice bush
   Was blooming round our feet;
Red hair she had and golden skin,
Her sulky lips were shaped for sin,
Her sturdy legs were flannel-slack'd,
The strongest legs in Pontefract.

The light and dangling licorice flowers
   Gave off the sweetest smells;
From various black Victorian towers
   The Sunday evening bells
Came pealing over dales and hills
And tanneries and silent mills
And lowly streets where country stops
And little shuttered corner shops.

She cast her blazing eyes on me
   And plucked a licorice leaf;
I was her captive slave and she
   My red-haired robber chief.
Oh love! for love I could not speak,
It left me winded, wilting, weak
And held in brown arms strong and bare
And wound with flaming ropes of hair.

Huxley Hall

In the Garden City Café with its murals on the wall
Before a talk on 'Sex and Civics' I meditated on the Fall.

Deep depression settled on me under that electric glare
While outside the lightsome poplars flanked the rose-beds in the
                                                        square.

While outside the carefree children sported in the summer haze
And released their inhibitions in a hundred different ways.

She who eats her greasy crumpets snugly in the inglenook
Of some birch-enshrouded homestead, dropping butter on her book

Can she know the deep depression of this bright, hygienic hell?
And her husband, stout free-thinker, can he share in it as well?

Not the folk-museum's charting of man's Progress out of slime
Can release me from the painful seeming accident of Time.

Barry smashes Shirley's dolly, Shirley's eyes are crossed with hate,
Comrades plot a Comrade's downfall 'in the interests of the State'.

Not my vegetarian dinner, not my lime-juice minus gin,
Quite can drown a faint conviction that we may be born in Sin.

House of Rest

Now all the world she knew is dead
  In this small room she lives her days
The wash-hand stand and single bed
  Screened from the public gaze.

The horse-brass shines, the kettle sings,
  The cup of China tea
Is tasted among cared-for things
  Ranged round for me to see –

Lincoln, by Valentine and Co.,
  Now yellowish brown and stained,
But there some fifty years ago
  Her Harry was ordained;

Outside the Church at Woodhall Spa
  The smiling groom and bride,
And here's his old tobacco jar
  Dried lavender inside.

I do not like to ask if he
  Was 'High' or 'Low' or 'Broad'
Lest such a question seem to be
  A mockery of Our Lord.

Her full grey eyes look far beyond
  The little room and me
To village church and village pond
  And ample rectory.

She sees her children each in place
    Eyes downcast as they wait,
She hears her Harry murmur Grace,
    Then heaps the porridge plate.

Aroused at seven, to bed by ten,
    They fully lived each day,
Dead sons, so motor-bike-mad then,
    And daughters far away.

Now when the bells for Eucharist
    Sound in the Market Square,
With sunshine struggling through the mist
    And Sunday in the air,

The veil between her and her dead
    Dissolves and shows them clear,
The Consecration Prayer is said
    And all of them are near.

Middlesex

Gaily into Ruislip Gardens
    Runs the red electric train,
With a thousand Ta's and Pardon's
    Daintily alights Elaine;
Hurries down the concrete station
With a frown of concentration,
Out into the outskirt's edges
Where a few surviving hedges
Keep alive our lost Elysium – rural Middlesex again.

Well cut Windsmoor flapping lightly,
    Jacqmar scarf of mauve and green
Hiding hair which, Friday nightly,
    Delicately drowns in Drene;
Fair Elaine the bobby-soxer,
Fresh-complexioned with Innoxa,
Gains the garden – father's hobby –
Hangs her Windsmoor in the lobby,
Settles down to sandwich supper and the television screen.

Gentle Brent, I used to know you
    Wandering Wembley-wards at will,
Now what change your waters show you
    In the meadowlands you fill!
Recollect the elm-trees misty
And the footpaths climbing twisty
Under cedar-shaded palings,
Low laburnum-leaned-on railings,
Out of Northolt on and upward to the heights of Harrow hill.

Parish of enormous hayfields
  Perivale stood all alone,
And from Greenford scent of mayfields
  Most enticingly was blown
Over market gardens tidy,
Taverns for the *bona fide*,
Cockney anglers, cockney shooters,
Murray Poshes, Lupin Pooters
Long in Kensal Green and Highgate silent under soot and stone.

Seaside Golf

How straight it flew, how long it flew,
   It clear'd the rutty track
And soaring, disappeared from view
   Beyond the bunker's back –
A glorious, sailing, bounding drive
That made me glad I was alive.

And down the fairway, far along
   It glowed a lonely white;
I played an iron sure and strong
   And clipp'd it out of sight,
And spite of grassy banks between
I knew I'd find it on the green.

And so I did. It lay content
   Two paces from the pin;
A steady putt and then it went
   Oh, most securely in.
The very turf rejoiced to see
That quite unprecedented three.

Ah! seaweed smells from sandy caves
   And thyme and mist in whiffs,
In-coming tide, Atlantic waves
   Slapping the sunny cliffs,
Lark song and sea sounds in the air
And splendour, splendour everywhere.

I.M.
Walter Ramsden
ob. March 26, 1947
Pembroke College, Oxford

Dr Ramsden cannot read *The Times* obituary today,
    He's dead.
Let monographs on silk worms by other people be
    Thrown away
    Unread
For he who best could understand and criticize them, he
    Lies clay
    In bed.

The body waits in Pembroke College where the ivy taps the panes
    All night;
That old head so full of knowledge, that good heart that kept the
                                   brains
    All right,
Those old cheeks that faintly flushed as the port suffused the veins,
    Drain'd white.

Crocus in the Fellows' Garden, winter jasmine up the wall
    Gleam gold.
Shadows of Victorian chimneys on the sunny grassplot fall
    Long, cold.
Master, Bursar, Senior Tutor, these, his three survivors, all
    Feel old.

They remember, as the coffin to its final obsequations
  Leaves the gates,
Buzz of bees in window boxes on their summer ministrations,
  Kitchen din,
  Cups and plates,
And the getting of bump suppers for the long-dead generations
  Coming in,
  From Eights.

Norfolk

How did the Devil come? When first attack?
  These Norfolk lanes recall lost innocence,
The years fall off and find me walking back
  Dragging a stick along the wooden fence
Down this same path, where, forty years ago,
My father strolled behind me, calm and slow.

I used to fill my hand with sorrel seeds
  And shower him with them from the tops of stiles,
I used to butt my head into his tweeds
  To make him hurry down those languorous miles
Of ash and alder-shaded lanes, till here
Our moorings and the masthead would appear.

There after supper lit by lantern light
  Warm in the cabin I could lie secure
And hear against the polished sides at night
  The lap lap lapping of the weedy Bure,
A whispering and watery Norfolk sound
Telling of all the moonlit reeds around.

How did the Devil come? When first attack?
  The church is just the same, though now I know
Fowler of Louth restored it. Time, bring back
  The rapturous ignorance of long ago,
The peace, before the dreadful daylight starts,
Of unkept promises and broken hearts.

The Metropolitan Railway

BAKER STREET STATION BUFFET

Early Electric! With what radiant hope
  Men formed this many-branched electrolier,
Twisted the flex around the iron rope
  And let the dazzling vacuum globes hang clear,
And then with hearts the rich contrivance fill'd
Of copper, beaten by the Bromsgrove Guild.

Early Electric! Sit you down and see,
  'Mid this fine woodwork and a smell of dinner,
A stained-glass windmill and a pot of tea,
  And sepia views of leafy lanes in PINNER, –
Then visualize, far down the shining lines,
Your parents' homestead set in murmuring pines.

Smoothly from HARROW, passing PRESTON ROAD,
  They saw the last green fields and misty sky,
At NEASDEN watched a workmen's train unload,
  And, with the morning villas sliding by,
They felt so sure on their electric trip
That Youth and Progress were in partnership.

And all that day in murky London Wall
  The thought of RUISLIP kept him warm inside;
At FARRINGDON that lunch hour at a stall
  He bought a dozen plants of London Pride;
While she, in arc-lit Oxford Street adrift,
Soared through the sales by safe hydraulic lift.

Early Electric! Maybe even here
   They met that evening at six-fifteen
Beneath the hearts of this electrolier
   And caught the first non-stop to WILLESDEN GREEN,
Then out and on, through rural RAYNER'S LANE
To autumn-scented Middlesex again.

Cancer has killed him. Heart is killing her.
   The trees are down. An Odeon flashes fire
Where stood their villa by the murmuring fir
   When 'they would for their children's good conspire'.
Of all their loves and hopes on hurrying feet
Thou art the worn memorial, Baker Street.

Sun and Fun

SONG OF A NIGHT-CLUB PROPRIETRESS

I walked into the night-club in the morning;
  There was kummel on the handle of the door.
The ashtrays were unemptied,
The cleaning unattempted,
  And a squashed tomato sandwich on the floor.

I pulled aside the thick magenta curtains
  – So Regency, so Regency, my dear –
And a host of little spiders
Ran a race across the ciders
  To a box of baby 'pollies by the beer.

Oh sun upon the summer-going by-pass
  Where ev'rything is speeding to the sea,
And wonder beyond wonder
That here where lorries thunder
  The sun should ever percolate to me.

When Boris used to call in his Sedanca,
  When Teddy took me down to his estate,
When my nose excited passion,
When my clothes were in the fashion,
  When my beaux were never cross if I was late,

There was sun enough for lazing upon beaches,
  There was fun enough for far into the night.
But I'm dying now and done for,
What on earth was all the fun for?
  For I'm old and ill and terrified and tight.

Original Sin on the Sussex Coast

Now on this out of season afternoon
Day schools which cater for the sort of boy
Whose parents go by Pullman once a month
To do a show in town, pour out their young
Into the sharply red October light.
Here where The Drive and Buckhurst Road converge
I watch the rival gangs and am myself
A schoolboy once again in shivering shorts.
I see the dust of sherbet on the chin
Of Andrew Knox well-dress'd, well-born, well-fed,
Even at nine a perfect gentleman,
Willie Buchanan waiting at his side –
Another Scot, eruptions on his skin.
I hear Jack Drayton whistling from the fence
Which hides the copper domes of 'Cooch Behar'.
That was the signal. So there's no escape.
A race for Willow Way and jump the hedge
Behind the Granville Bowling Club? Too late.
They'll catch me coming out in Seapink Lane.
Across the Garden of Remembrance? No,
That would be blasphemy and bring bad luck.
Well then, I'm *for* it. Andrew's at me first,
He pinions me in that especial grip
His brother learned in Kobë from a Jap
(No chance for me against the Japanese).
Willie arrives and winds me with a punch
Plumb in the tummy, grips the other arm.
'You're to be booted. Hold him steady, chaps!'
A wait for taking aim. Oh trees and sky!
Then crack against the column of my spine,
Blackness and breathlessness and sick with pain
I stumble on the asphalt. Off they go

Away, away, thank God, and out of sight
So that I lie quite still and climb to sense
Too out of breath and strength to make a sound.
  Now over Polegate vastly sets the sun;
Dark rise the Downs from darker looking elms,
And out of Southern railway trains to tea
Run happy boys down various Station Roads,
Satchels of homework jogging on their backs,
So trivial and so healthy in the shade
Of these enormous Downs. And when they're home,
When the Post-Toasties mixed with Golden Shred
Make for the kiddies such a scrumptious feast,
Does Mum, the Persil-user, still believe
That there's no Devil and that youth is bliss?
As certain as the sun behind the Downs
And quite as plain to see, the Devil walks.

Devonshire Street W.1

The heavy mahogany door with its wrought-iron screen
   Shuts. And the sound is rich, sympathetic, discreet.
The sun still shines on this eighteenth-century scene
   With Edwardian faience adornments – Devonshire Street.

No hope. And the X-ray photographs under his arm
   Confirm the message. His wife stands timidly by.
The opposite brick-built house looks lofty and calm
   Its chimneys steady against a mackerel sky.

No hope. And the iron knob of this palisade
   So cold to the touch, is luckier now than he
'Oh merciless, hurrying Londoners! Why was I made
   For the long and the painful deathbed coming to me?'

She puts her fingers in his as, loving and silly,
   At long-past Kensington dances she used to do
'It's cheaper to take the tube to Piccadilly
   And then we can catch a nineteen or a twenty-two.'

Business Girls

From the geyser ventilators
  Autumn winds are blowing down
On a thousand business women
  Having baths in Camden Town.

Waste pipes chuckle into runnels,
  Steam's escaping here and there,
Morning trains through Camden cutting
  Shake the Crescent and the Square.

Early nip of changeful autumn,
  Dahlias glimpsed through garden doors,
At the back precarious bathrooms
  Jutting out from upper floors;

And behind their frail partitions
  Business women lie and soak,
Seeing through the draughty skylight
  Flying clouds and railway smoke.

Rest you there, poor unbelov'd ones,
  Lap your loneliness in heat.
All too soon the tiny breakfast,
  Trolley-bus and windy street!

The Old Liberals

Pale green of the *English Hymnal*! Yattendon hymns
   Played on the *hautbois* by a lady dress'd in blue
   Her white-hair'd father accompanying her thereto
On tenor or bass-recorder. Daylight swims
   On sectional bookcase, delicate cup and plate
   And William de Morgan tiles around the grate
And many the silver birches the pearly light shines through.

I think such a running together of woodwind sound,
   Such painstaking piping high on a Berkshire hill,
   Is sad as an English autumn heavy and still,
Sad as a country silence, tractor-drowned;
   For deep in the hearts of the man and the woman playing
   The rose of a world that was not has withered away.
Where are the wains with garlanded swathes a-swaying?
Where are the swains to wend through the lanes a-maying?
   Where are the blithe and jocund to ted the hay?
   Where are the free folk of England? Where are they?

Ask of the Abingdon bus with full load creeping
   Down into denser suburbs. The birch lets go
   But one brown leaf upon browner bracken below.
Ask of the cinema manager. Night airs die
To still, ripe scent of the fungus and wet woods weeping.
   Ask at the fish and chips in the Market Square.
   Here amid firs and a final sunset flare
Recorder and *hautbois* only moan at a mouldering sky.

Hunter Trials

It's awf'lly bad luck on Diana,
 Her ponies have swallowed their bits;
She fished down their throats with a spanner
 And frightened them all into fits.

So now she's attempting to borrow.
 Do lend her some bits, Mummy, *do*;
I'll lend her my own for tomorrow,
 But today *I*'ll be wanting them too.

Just look at Prunella on Guzzle,
 The wizardest pony on earth;
Why doesn't she slacken his muzzle
 And tighten the breech in his girth?

I say, Mummy, there's Mrs Geyser
 And doesn't she look pretty sick?
I bet it's because Mona Lisa
 Was hit on the hock with a brick.

Miss Blewitt says Monica threw it,
 But Monica says it was Joan,
And Joan's very thick with Miss Blewitt,
 So Monica's sulking alone.

And Margaret failed in her paces,
 Her withers got tied in a noose,
So her coronets caught in the traces
 And now all her fetlocks are loose.

Oh, it's me now. I'm terribly nervous.
  I wonder if Smudges will shy.
She's practically certain to swerve as
  Her Pelham is over one eye.

*   *   *

Oh wasn't it naughty of Smudges?
  Oh, Mummy, I'm sick with disgust.
She threw me in front of the Judges,
  And my silly old collarbone's bust.

How to Get On in Society

Originally set as a competition in *Time and Tide*

Phone for the fish-knives, Norman
   As Cook is a little unnerved;
You kiddies have crumpled the serviettes
   And I must have things daintily served.

Are the requisites all in the toilet?
   The frills round the cutlets can wait
Till the girl has replenished the cruets
   And switched on the logs in the grate.

It's ever so close in the lounge, dear,
   But the vestibule's comfy for tea
And Howard is out riding on horseback
   So do come and take some with me.

Now here is a fork for your pastries
   And do use the couch for your feet;
I know what I wanted to ask you –
   Is trifle sufficient for sweet?

Milk and then just as it comes dear?
   I'm afraid the preserve's full of stones;
Beg pardon, I'm soiling the doilies
   With afternoon tea-cakes and scones.

False Security

I remember the dread with which I at a quarter past four
Let go with a bang behind me our house front door
And, clutching a present for my dear little hostess tight,
Sailed out for the children's party into the night
Or rather the gathering night. For still some boys
In the near municipal acres were making a noise
Shuffling in fallen leaves and shouting and whistling
And running past hedges of hawthorn, spiky and bristling.
And black in the oncoming darkness stood out the trees
And pink shone the ponds in the sunset ready to freeze
And all was still and ominous waiting for dark
And the keeper was ringing his closing bell in the park
And the arc lights started to fizzle and burst into mauve
As I climbed West Hill to the great big house in The Grove,
Where the children's party was and the dear little hostess.
But halfway up stood the empty house where the ghost is.
I crossed to the other side and under the arc
Made a rush for the next kind lamp-post out of the dark
And so to the next and the next till I reached the top
Where the Grove branched off to the left. Then ready to drop
I ran to the ironwork gateway of number seven
Secure at last on the lamplit fringe of Heaven.
Oh who can say how subtle and safe one feels
Shod in one's children's sandals from Daniel Neal's,
Clad in one's party clothes made of stuff from Heal's?
And who can still one's thrill at the candle shine
On cakes and ices and jelly and blackcurrant wine,
And the warm little feel of my hostess's hand in mine?
Can I forget my delight at the conjuring show?
And wasn't I proud that I was the last to go?
Too overexcited and pleased with myself to know

That the words I heard my hostess's mother employ
To a guest departing, would ever diminish my joy,
I WONDER WHERE JULIA FOUND THAT STRANGE, RATHER
COMMON LITTLE BOY?

Thoughts on 'The Diary of a Nobody'

The Pooters walked to Watney Lodge
　　One Sunday morning hot and still
Where public footpaths used to dodge
　　Round elms and oaks to Muswell Hill.

That burning buttercuppy day
　　The local dogs were curled in sleep,
The writhing trunks of flowery May
　　Were polished by the sides of sheep.

And only footsteps in a lane
　　And birdsong broke the silence round
And chuffs of the Great Northern train
　　For Alexandra Palace bound.

The Watney Lodge I seem to see
　　Is gabled gothic hard and red,
With here a monkey puzzle tree
　　And there a round geranium bed.

Each mansion, each new-planted pine,
　　Each short and ostentatious drive
Meant Morning Prayer and beef and wine
　　And Queen Victoria alive.

Dear Charles and Carrie, I am sure,
　　Despite that awkward Sunday dinner,
Your lives were good and more secure
　　Than ours at cocktail time in Pinner.

Felixstowe, *or*
The Last of Her Order

With one consuming roar along the shingle
    The long wave claws and rakes the pebbles down
To where its backwash and the next wave mingle,
    A mounting arch of water weedy-brown
Against the tide the off-shore breezes blow.
Oh wind and water, this is Felixstowe.

In winter when the sea winds chill and shriller
    Than those of summer, all their cold unload
Full on the gimcrack attic of the villa
    Where I am lodging off the Orwell Road,
I put my final shilling in the meter
And only make my loneliness completer.

In eighteen ninety-four when we were founded,
    Counting our Reverend Mother we were six,
How full of hope we were and prayer-surrounded
    'The Little Sisters of the Hanging Pyx'.
We built our orphanage. We ran our school.
Now only I am left to keep the rule.

Here in the gardens of the Spa Pavilion
    Warm in the whisper of a summer sea,
The cushioned scabious, a deep vermilion,
    With white pins stuck in it, looks up at me
A sun-lit kingdom touched by butterflies
And so my memory of winter dies.

Across the grass the poplar shades grow longer
  And louder clang the waves along the coast.
The band packs up. The evening breeze is stronger
  And all the world goes home to tea and toast.
I hurry past a cakeshop's tempting scones
Bound for the red brick twilight of St John's.

'Thou knowest my down sitting and mine uprising'
  Here where the white light burns with steady glow
Safe from the vain world's silly sympathizing,
  Safe with the Love that I was born to know,
Safe from the surging of the lonely sea
My heart finds rest, my heart finds rest in Thee.

A Bay in Anglesey

The sleepy sound of a tea-time tide
Slaps at the rocks the sun has dried,

Too lazy, almost, to sink and lift
Round low peninsulas pink with thrift.

The water, enlarging shells and sand,
Grows greener emerald out from land

And brown over shadowy shelves below
The waving forests of seaweed show.

Here at my feet in the short cliff grass
Are shells, dried bladderwrack, broken glass,

Pale blue squills and yellow rock roses.
The next low ridge that we climb discloses

One more field for the sheep to graze
While, scarcely seen on this hottest of days,

Far to the eastward, over there,
Snowdon rises in pearl-grey air.

Multiple lark-song, whispering bents,
The thymy, turfy and salty scents

And filling in, brimming in, sparkling and free
The sweet susurration of incoming sea.

Uffington

Tonight we feel the muffled peal
   Hang on the village like a pall;
It overwhelms the towering elms –
   That death-reminding dying fall;
The very sky no longer high
   Comes down within the reach of all.
Imprisoned in a cage of sound
Even the trivial seems profound.

The Hon. Sec.

The flag that hung half-mast today
    Seemed animate with being
As if it knew for whom it flew
    And will no more be seeing.

He loved each corner of the links –
    The stream at the eleventh,
The grey-green bents, the pale sea-pinks,
    The prospect from the seventh;

To the ninth tee the uphill climb,
    A grass and sandy stairway,
And at the top the scent of thyme
    And long extent of fairway.

He knew how on a summer day
    The sea's deep blue grew deeper,
How evening shadows over Bray
    Made that round hill look steeper.

He knew the ocean mists that rose
    And seemed for ever staying,
When moaned the foghorn from Trevose
    And nobody was playing;

The flip of cards on winter eves,
    The whisky and the scoring,
As trees outside were stripped of leaves
    And heavy seas were roaring.

He died when early April light
  Showed red his garden sally
And under pale green spears glowed white
  His lilies of the valley:

That garden where he used to stand
  And where the robin waited
To fly and perch upon his hand
  And feed till it was sated.

The Times would never have the space
  For Ned's discreet achievements;
The public prints are not the place
  For intimate bereavements.

A gentle guest, a willing host,
  Affection deeply planted –
It's strange that those we miss the most
  Are those we take for granted.

Monody on the Death
of a Platonist Bank Clerk

This is the lamp where he first read Whitman
 Out of the library large and free.
Every quarter the bus to Kirkstall
 Stopped and waited, but on read he.

This was his room with books in plenty:
 Dusty, now I have raised the blind –
Fenimore Cooper, Ballantyne, Henty,
 Edward Carpenter wedged behind.

These are the walls adorned with portraits,
 Camera studies and Kodak snaps;
'Camp at Pevensey' – 'Scouts at Cleethorpes' –
 There he is with the lads and chaps.

This is the friend, the best and greatest,
 Pure in his surplice, smiling, true –
The enlarged Photomaton – that's the latest,
 Next to the coloured one 'August Blue'.

These are his pipes. Ah! how he loved them,
 Puffed and petted them, after walks,
After tea and a frowst with crumpets,
 Puffed the smoke into serious talks.

All the lot of them, how they came to him –
 Tea and chinwag – gay young lives!
Somehow they were never the same to him
 When they married and brought their wives.

Executive

I am a young executive. No cuffs than mine are cleaner;
I have a Slimline brief-case and I use the firm's Cortina.
In every roadside hostelry from here to Burgess Hill
The *maîtres d'hôtel* all know me well and let me sign the bill.

You ask me what it is I do. Well actually, you know,
I'm partly a liaison man and partly P.R.O.
Essentially I integrate the current export drive
And basically I'm viable from ten o'clock till five.

For vital off-the-record work – that's talking transport-wise –
I've a scarlet Aston-Martin – and does she go? She flies!
Pedestrians and dogs and cats – we mark them down for slaughter.
I also own a speed-boat which has never touched the water.

She's built of fibre-glass, of course. I call her 'Mandy Jane'
After a bird I used to know – No soda, please, just plain –
And how did I acquire her? Well to tell you about that
And to put you in the picture I must wear my other hat.

I do some mild developing. The sort of place I need
Is a quiet country market town that's rather run to seed.
A luncheon and a drink or two, a little *savoir faire* –
I fix the Planning Officer, the Town Clerk and the Mayor.

And if some preservationist attempts to interfere
A 'dangerous structure' notice from the Borough Engineer
Will settle any buildings that are standing in our way –
The modern style, sir, with respect, has really come to stay.

Back from Australia

Cocooned in Time, at this inhuman height,
    The packaged food tastes neutrally of clay.
    We never seem to catch the running day
But travel on in everlasting night
With all the chic accoutrements of flight:
    Lotions and essences in neat array
    And yet another plastic cup and tray.
'Thank you *so* much. Oh no, I'm quite all right.'

At home in Cornwall hurrying autumn skies
    Leave Bray Hill barren, Stepper jutting bare,
        And hold the moon above the sea-wet sand.
The very last of late September dies
    In frosty silence and the hills declare
        How vast the sky is, looked at from the land.

Inland Waterway

[Declaimed at the opening of the Upper Avon at Stratford in the
presence of the Queen Mother and Robert Aickman, founder of the
Inland Waterways Association, on 1 June 1974.]

He who by peaceful inland water steers
Bestirs himself when a new lock appears.
Slow swing the gates: slow sinks the water down;
This lower Stratford seems another town.
The meadows which the youthful Shakespeare knew
Are left behind, and, sliding into view,
Come reaches of the Avon, mile on mile,
Church, farm and mill and lover-leaned-on stile,
Till where the tower of Tewkesbury soars to heaven
Our homely Avon joins the haughty Severn.
Sweet is the fluting of the blackbird's note,
Sweet is the ripple from the narrow boat.

Your Majesty, our friend of many years,
Confirms a triumph now the moment nears;
The lock you have re-opened will set free
The heart of England to the open sea.

Chelsea 1977

The street was bathed in winter sunset pink
The air was redolent of kitchen sink
Between the dog-mess heaps I picked my way
To watch the dying embers of the day
Glow over Chelsea, crimson load on load
All Brangwynesque across the long King's Road.
Deep in myself I felt a sense of doom
Fearful of death I trudge towards the tomb.
The earth beneath my feet is hardly soil
But outstretched chicken-netting coil on coil
Covering cables, sewage-pipes and wires
While underneath burn hell's eternal fires.
Snap, crackle! pop! the kiddiz know the sound
And Satan stokes his furnace underground.

Summer

(Written at the age of thirteen and a half, as a task for 'prep', and published in The Draconian, *the magazine of the Dragon School.)*

Whatever will rhyme with Summer?
There only is 'plumber' and 'drummer':
Why! the cleverest bard
Would find it quite hard
To connect with the Summer – a plumber!

My Mind's getting glummer and glummer
Hooray! there's a word besides drummer;
Oh, I will think of some
Ere the prep's end has come
But the rhymes will get rummer and rummer.

Ah! If the bee hums, it's a hummer;
And the bee showeth signs of the Summer;
Also holiday babels
Make th'porter gum labels,
And whenever he gums, he's a gummer!

The cuckoo's a goer and comer
He goes in the hot days of Summer;
But he cucks ev'ry day
Till you plead and you pray
That his voice will get dumber and dumber!

Part Two · Prose

Lord Mount Prospect

I

Whenever I sit down to my solitary meal of an evening, I am put in mind of the many obscure Irish peers who are sitting down to theirs. Some, perhaps, in a room over the stables, gaze at the moonlit ruins of what once was a stately mansion; others sip port as the Adam decoration peels off the ceiling and falls with an accustomed thud to the floor. The wind sighs and sings through the lonely Irish night round the wet walls of every house and down each grass-grown drive until it causes even the stable bell to tinkle, although the clock has long ago ceased to work. Such thoughts as these divert me, and such thoughts as these produced the narrative which I am about to relate.

It was after a dinner where the food and the wine and the guests were well selected, where there was an absence of academic friction and where an aromatic content had settled in upon us, that the germ of an important society came into being. Did we not follow a tradition handed down in our universities by Wesley, Heber, Tennyson and Wilde? The Society for the Discovery of Obscure Peers was militantly charitable from its outset. It was produced in the glow caused by good food and drink, it was later to burst with good intentions that would fall on Ireland like golden rain. A desultory conversation upon the acute condition of that country had led up to speculations upon its grander inhabitants. There was that comforting lightness about the talk which unites the intelligent.

How kind it would be, we considered, if we were to arrange a dinner for the obscurer Irish peers! It was very sensibly suggested that some of them might not be able to afford the fare to England, so that a meal in their own country should be arranged, if their own country could provide it. With such a spirit of unselfishness the Society was formed, an example not so much of the waste of talent and pettifogging machinations of the pedant as of the oblique large-heartedness that typifies a university. The following rules, unwritten but telling, were composed:

1. *Who's Who* shall be accepted as the truth.

2. Any distinction, regarded by the Society as distinguished, disqualifies the peer. This rule would not affect, for instance, Lord Pentagon, who states in *Who's Who* that he is vice-Chairman of the Ballysligo Branch of the Church of Ireland Jubilee Fund Administrative Committee.

3. A peer who is known to a member of the Society is disqualified.

4. A younger brother or son and heir does not count.

The method of selecting an object for our charity was similar to that used by those with simple faith in the Bible, who have no doubts about the minor prophets. *Who's Who* was opened at random. The nearest peer who conformed to the Society's rules was chosen, and every effort was made to get into touch with him.

The usual device was to write and say we were interested in electrical matters and proposed erecting a plant on his estate. This plan was abandoned after the trouble with Lord Octagon. He replied on crimson note-paper and said he would be delighted to see his correspondent.

Our member set out for the west of Ireland. Octagon Abbey was a glorious extravaganza of the eighteenth century. Within it sat Lord Octagon, surrounded by Indian relics collected by his ancestors and by himself. At great expense he had had electric eels imported into his own fish-ponds. His knowledge of electricity was amazing. With fanatical fervour he explained his device for breeding the eels and conserving their electricity by means of a plant which he intended to establish at the edge of the ponds. It was three months before Lord Octagon could be induced to abandon the scheme, three months of anxiety for members, both at home and abroad.

Then there was the other plan of introduction: 'Would you be so good as to allow me to consult your library, where I believe there are some valuable sixteenth-century editions of Vergil?' Lord Santry, who is one of our staunchest supporters, replied in the kindest way. He welcomed the request of the member chosen for the task. Soon after his arrival at Cahir Santry, our member was informed of his host's translation of the libretto of all the Savoy operas into Latin hexameters. The first three volumes have cost the Society more than it can reasonably be expected to pay.

I suppose we had collected something like ninety peers and were considering the extension of our membership in order that a successful dinner might be provided when the problem of Lord Mount Prospect arose.

It was not usual for our letters to be disregarded. Persons as lonely as the objects of our charity become excited even on the receipt of an advertisement. For weeks and weeks they gaze out of their castles at the surrounding swamp, unable, probably, to reach the nearest village owing to the torrents of rain and the floods which mirror the leaden sky. Then, when summer comes, and with it a ray of sunlight, they are overjoyed to get a letter from the outside world.

But not so Lord Mount Prospect. The *Who's Who* was loose in the binding and the pages torn and thumbed like a directory outside a public telephone box when we discovered his name. In truth, the mission of the Society was nearly accomplished; there were few obscure peers left, and the fervour and charity which had started our project was waning under disillusion. For the most part our peers were happy in their gloomy mansions, they showed real pleasure as the footman brought in the oil lamps and they could settle down to a long evening of cutting out jig-saw puzzles or pasting halfpenny stamps on to a fire-screen.

We were, then, somewhat disappointed to find the name of Lord Mount Prospect: but even the most lukewarm among us was stimulated by the odd way in which he announced himself.

MOUNT PROSPECT (10th Vis:), cr: 1684. Archibald Standish CosPatrick Reeve, b: 1849. An Ember Day Bryanite. Address: Mount Prospect, County Galway.

What is an Ember Day Bryanite? With trembling hands we turned to Haydn's *Dictionary of Dates*. Allow me to quote from Haydn's *Dictionary of Dates* (1871):

EMBER DAY BRYANITES is the name given to an obscure sect which was founded by William Bryan, a tailor of Paternoster Row, London, and his cousin, John Reeve, a chandler in the city of Exeter. These two declared to the world in 1717 that they were the two witnesses mentioned in Rev. xi, 3. 'And I will give power unto my two witnesses and they shall prophesy a thousand, two hundred and three-score days, clothed in sackcloth.' They hold many curious beliefs, among which the chief is that God came down in person on to the cross and left Elijah as vice-regent in Heaven. They believe in a bodily resurrection and the sleep of the soul. They declare that the sun is four miles from the earth. The sect was still in existence, according to the census, in 1851.

That spirit of research and curiosity which made possible the forthcoming adventure prompted me to visit a deserted part of north London during the autumn of last year. Could it be that Ember Day Bryanites were still prophesying away up the Caledonian Road? Could it be that even now tired charwomen and weary tailors dressed themselves in sackcloth to listen? Under 'Places of Worship' in the *London Directory* I wondered at the hopeful signs I found. Last and almost least, beneath 'Other Denominations', below the Particular Baptists, and the Peculiar People, below the Sandemanians and Independent Calvinistics, came the glorious words, 'Ember Day Bryanite', and the address, 'Hungerford Green, Barnsbury, N.1.'

Fortified with a long and beautiful lunch which lasted until the time when the others have tea, I trod out into the Sunday evening. There was a waiting hush about the Gothic Revival steeples which pricked the starlit London sky: the well-lit thrills of evensong were hardly in preparation, and electric light had not yet thrown up the full richness of nineteenth-century glass which was to stream on to the pavement without.

But what a change met my eye as I left the black brick station, vast and deserted, near the Caledonian Road and saw the fervour of north London's religious life! Above the noise of tram-car bells, above the gear-changing of the cheaper motor-cars, for this day no longer commercial, and back from the deep joys of Epping and Chingford, above the rich peal of a parish church and the insistent tinkle of a chapel-of-ease urgently in need of funds could be heard quavering sopranos and the Cockney hoarseness of men and women pronouncing a warning of the wrath to come. There they stood, amid listless little groups, gathered inside turnings off the main road. Some political, many religious, and most neither the one nor the other but vaguely connected with anti-vivisection or the suppression of the Jews, they prophesied with equal fervour of a doom hanging perilously near us.

Small wonder that my progress was slow towards the pleasant little hill embellished with low stucco houses that led up to Hungerford Green! Small wonder that I almost changed my mind as I caught the bright eyes of a thin bearded gentleman proving the inevitability of another deluge. The silence of the empty streets upon the hill enveloped me with the uneasy comfort of a blanket. Only the knowledge of my curious goal urged me on.

Hungerford Green was attractive enough. It was a relic of successful Regency commerce. Two-storeyed houses, once 'tight boxes, neatly sashed', surrounded an oblong space of burnt grass with a curious pavilion in the middle, some conceit of a former merchant aping the gazebos of the great and good. The railings round the grass were sadly bent to make loop-holes for dogs and children, the noble urns of ironwork were battered: from all over Hungerford Green came the whooping of hymns loud enough to stream through ventilating spaces in the pointed windows of Baptist and Wesleyan chapel. The worn grass was bright with the rays of gas-light from the places of worship, with an additional brightness from the outside lamp of a more prosperous chapel where electric light had been installed.

Joyous opening strains of a hearty Nonconformist service! How anxious was I to know under what gas or electric light Ember Day Bryanites, possibly in sackcloth, were even now praising the Lord! And so, reining my enthusiasm with happy delay, I asked a girl whether she knew which was the chapel of the Ember Day Bryanites. She burst into those whooping shrieks maid-servants affect on a roundabout. A sympathetic but dreary woman beside her, yellower and more miserable, suggested that perhaps I meant the Baptist Chapel. When I replied that I did not, a sad, long, nasal negative streamed out of her mouth and nose.

With no faint heart I walked round the green, yet fearful of breaking silence with irreligious feet, and I scanned the names on black and gilded notice-boards. 'Congregational', 'Primitive Methodist', 'United Methodist', 'New Jerusalem', 'Presbyterian

Church of England', and the last was the last of the lighted chapels which made glorious Hungerford Green. It could not be that the directory was wrong or that my eyes had betrayed me.

There in the remotest corner of the place was the black pedimented outline of an enormous building, more like a warehouse than anything else. As I approached I saw a space of green before it boldly sheltering a struggling plane tree. But the gates of the pathway were padlocked, and a street lamp showed that the path was almost grass. No light or sound came from the great edifice in front, the hymns of the neighbouring chapels had died down to spontaneous prayer, and only the Sunday roar of north London disturbed the air.

I scaled the rusty railing that protected the grass before the chapel building. The plot was bigger and darker than I had supposed, and the chapel loomed so large and high on my approach that it was almost as if it had moved forward to interrupt me. It was plain and square, with a coating of plaster which had peeled in many places and fallen on to the untidy grass below.

I could just discern a printed notice about an electoral roll, years old and clinging limply to its inefficient paste. The double rows of windows were bolted and boarded up. The great doors were shut. But beside them was a wooden notice-board with the remains of lettering still upon it. I struck a match and read:

THOSE WHO ARE CHOSEN FOR HIS
COURTS ABOVE WILL MEET HERE
(GOD WILLING) ON THE LORD'S
DAY AT 11 A.M. AND AT 6.30.
Holy Supper by Arrangement.

The Lord had received His Ember Day Bryanites.

2

Meanwhile the Society had not been idle in its attempts to form an acquaintanceship with Lord Mount Prospect, nor had it failed to follow them with experiments more daring. The silence of his Lordship and the mystery which surrounded his name made even the idea of his existence uncertain. A member had written, after a careful study of the geological and political maps of County Galway, professing an interest in the peat bog which extended for some miles round Mount Prospect. His personal and delicately worded letter had evinced no reply. Undeterred by this he had stolen some paper from the *Methodist Recorder* and written to suggest a union of the Methodist and Ember Day Bryanite churches. He had been equally unsuccessful.

Notwithstanding, he conceived a bolder proposition. It is a general rule that Irish peers are interested in natural history; at considerable expense and with no little trouble, a large rhinoceros, stuffed and redecorated during the latter part of the last century, was moved with little regret from the spacious hall of a member's country mansion. It was packed by a firm which was intimately connected with the Natural History Museum, and transported to Ireland. The duty levied by the Free State Government was enormous.

Three months later the rhinoceros was returned. The workmen had been unable to find the road to Mount Prospect and had wandered about Galway for the greater part of a fortnight. Being English they found it hard to get into communication with the inhabitants. When they finally discovered the way to Lord Mount Prospect's estate they were unable to reach it.

Although it was high summer (the flies and the other insects must have been unpleasant, while even the peat bogs must have been withered in their very channels), the swamps around Mount Prospect were impassable. In a letter, the contractors attempted to describe, in what terms commercial language will allow, the state of things which their employees had encountered. There were large bridges along the road which had either been blown up in the 'trouble' or fallen into ruin; vehicular traffic had not been known to go to his lordship's estate within the memory of the said natives, and so the firm regretted inability *re* animal as per contract and would beg to return the same to hand.

The news of the final extinction of the Ember Day Bryanites in London, which I was able to bring before the Society, filled all with gloom and disappointment, but it did not quench the reawakened ardour. A letter was sent to every obscure peer befriended by the

Society, seeking information, in a tactful manner, of Lord Mount Prospect. Only three had heard his name, none had seen him, and only one supplied information. This was Lord Octagon, whose tales were clearly untrue.

We pictured fearful scenes in the silent mansion of Mount Prospect – a skeleton sitting in a ruined dining-room grinning over a now very aged glass of port, a corpse rotting between sheets of coroneted Irish linen.

The natural course was to go to the *Daily Express* and suggest a 'scoop', which would at the same time replenish the funds of the Society. A lord who was the very reverse of all that we stood for kindly undertook the unearthing of Lord Mount Prospect. For a week he was mentioned in the social columns. The Dragoman saw him at Tooth's Galleries looking at a fascinating exhibition of the etchings of the insides of railway engines by Frank Brangwyn. He met him at a party in St John's Wood where everyone was dressed as a clergyman, later in the same evening he met him at another party where everyone was dressed as a policeman.

Possibly some of my readers may remember what happened after this. He was removed to the front page of the paper. He had been about to make an ascent in a balloon from Sydenham when he was kidnapped. 'THE MISSING PEER' was billed all over London for three days. But the 'scoop' failed. No reply came from Lord Mount Prospect, safe in his castle in Ireland.

The wet weather had by now settled down and it was hopeless to attempt the journey through Galway until the next summer. At Christmas a present of handkerchiefs was sent, purporting to come from a poor relation in Harringay. But it, too, met with no response. After this the practical efforts of the Society ceased until next year should render personal investigation possible.

3

> Oh! *My* prestidigitation
> Is the bulwark of the nation
> And *I* like *my* new creation
> As Mi-Lord High Conjurer-er-er.

CHORUS:

Oh! *His* prestidigitation
Is the bulwark of the nation
And *he* likes *his* new creation
   As The Lord High Conjurer-er-er-er-er.

With an irregular rattling the persons behind the scenes tugged the curtain across the stage. The applause was deafening and for the fifth time the curtain was pulled apart; and for the last time, for the temporary nature of the fittings had caused it to stick, and there stood the actors, sweat glistening through their grease paint, their smiles happy.

There was a renewed burst of clapping; the spirit of fun was not dead yet. For a sixth, seventh and up to an eleventh time the enraptured audience called for an encore of that wonderful final chorus. The curtains stood ominously apart. The humourless stage manager turned out the lights on the stage. Peers and their wives in the front, army men, clergymen and their families in the back, retained the calm of good breeding until the lights were switched on in the hall.

We had known that Gilbert and Sullivan would work miracles. The exquisite humour of that last chorus of the *Bunundrum*, where the hero becomes Chief Conjuror in the land of Og-a-gog after all that trouble with the wicked emperor, the sense of satire and kindly irony that runs through the whole play, the clean wit not unworthy of the pages of *Punch*, and the perfect poetry of some of the serious bits which show that Gilbert could write serious stuff as well, make the *Bunundrum* one of the best of the Savoy operas. Of course, like them all, it has been repeated daily ever since 1888; but it does not lose by repetition. No great works of art do, do they?

4

The clouds were lying low but not unpleasantly over the peat bog, and a traveller might have descried, sandwiched between the clouds and the brown earth, little figures delving and hurrying. Were he to have approached closer he would have seen that the figures were of people obviously clever. Some wore spectacles and little-used cricket shirts, others had bought their ties in Paris.

The road to Mount Prospect was being repaired. The funds of the Society, replenished by the Gilbert and Sullivan performance, had paid for a thoroughly successful dinner for obscure peers which was held in the Shelburne Hotel in Dublin. The speeches were rather long.

With the money left over we were able to hire implements and horses. Like Ruskin we set to work to build a road. The track climbed a slight hill after many miles along the flat bog, and lying below it we saw a black pool whose water was strangely still. The silence was intensified by a sound as of distant applause too half-hearted for Gilbert and Sullivan. It was water lapping and licking the granite on the hillside shore of the pool. This edge was white with the powder of the ground stone, ground by ages of black water. The remaining shores were of reeds and meadow-sweet, which disappeared into a blue and distant hill.

Mount Prospect at last in view! Eagerly we stumbled down the declivity of the shore of the lake, and there it was that a surprise unnerved us. This nether shore was littered with paper, so that it might well have been a Surrey beauty spot, and only when we examined the paper closely did we discover that it was not. Thousands of unopened envelopes and parcels lay everywhere. Upon them 'Viscount Mount Prospect' was written in the fading hands of many generations. Someone discovered a package less sodden than most others and battered by but one year's Christmas storms. It was just possible to read the word Harringay on the postmark, while within, the dye had not yet come off six cheap pocket handkerchiefs.

As we were discussing how to cross the lake and the marsh beyond it to where the blue hill swam, a Zion, before our eyes, a postman, black against the skyline, emptied a solitary letter down the slope.

For over a week the sound of hammers and axes resounded on the shore of the black lake. A flat-bottomed boat was built, slim yet not ungainly, and a happy band paddled away in it down the stream that led out of all that black water.

For many hours the weeds and rushes were too high to give a view of the landscape. The dark water writhed with tentacles of water-weed undisturbed for, probably, more than a century. The stream twisted so abruptly, enclosing us in tall prisons of reed, black water and grey sky, that conversation was awed into silence, broken by the bravado of community singing.

Now and then we went up backwaters and had to turn, and once we were confronted with a broken bridge in a style formerly Indian, now decayed beyond repair. Here and there, swans, more wild than the wildest of song and story, rushed hissing and flapping on our little party from the dark deep bends of the stream, possibly angered by the community singing. The lights were long among some tattered beech trees when we moored our boat beside the Taj Mahal.

But is the Taj Mahal covered with pink stucco? And are there curious Gothic pinnacles behind it? Has the central dome collapsed so that it looks like a diseased onion? Is there grass along the avenues? And if there are beech trees and box hedges around the Taj Mahal, are they overgrown and straggling?

So long as the lingering day lasted we trod among the deserted courtyards and sparsely furnished rooms – incongruously Adam and Chippendale within – whose fittings and mildewed portraits, whose hangings and crumbling walls, whose awful silence was stirred only by the hum of a late fly, the squeak of a bat or the little ticking noises of hurrying beetles. Nowhere was there sign of living person or lifeless corpse. This was Ireland indeed. This was a romantic and poetical finale to a beautiful story. Lord Mount Prospect did not exist. He had been caught up in a bodily resurrection to sit for ever with other Ember Day Bryanites.

Such were our thoughts, and such they would have remained had we not entered what we had taken to be the back of the house, but which turned out to be but another front. Genius of optical illusions, you eighteenth-century builder! What appeared to be the Taj Mahal on one side was like a very rough sketch of the west front of Peterborough Cathedral on the other. It, too, was pink, in order that the sun might always appear to be setting across pinnacle and crocket.

A vast door showed us the way into a bare chapel with walls of dim

Pompeian red. The building was lit by frosted glass fixed into windows boldly representing the pointed style. Never was there so much dust. Yet the eyes involuntarily turned to the pulpit, placed, as in all chapels, where the altar rests in a papistical church.

In the dim light we could see that this plain wooden pulpit, raised above the rows of empty pews, was a welter of papers, piled up to the very sounding board and encumbering the winding staircase. Then – oh! horror! – a black-gowned figure, whose head was a skull off which all but the spectacles had withered, whose arm rested on a pile of papers, and whose fleshless finger kept a place – a dumb, still, black-gowned figure was propped upright against the papers.

Some time passed of clicking silence before anyone ventured near the sight. When the bravest did so, it was only to see that the papers were all a discourse, and that the fingers rested at the phrase 'and three thousand, two hundred and thirty secondly . . .' Lord Mount Prospect has preached his longest sermon and the mourners go about the streets.

Motopolis

Evening in Oxford was the romantic time. The bells would ring for evening chapel from all the colleges, dim or important, those churches under the influence of the Tractarians would tinkle out a call to evensong, there would be a noise at the boathouses along the Cherwell of punts being moored to the bank and the 'plop' of heavy feet walking away along the duckboards, the sun would go down behind the spires and towers, and artists would put the glory into their water-colours, gowned figures would hurry through cloisters, and white choirs would file into the candlelight. The bells would die down, and the University would thank God for another day, well spent, before the serious drinking began.

Now, though the bells ring, you cannot hear them above the motor-bicycles and gear-changing. As for the drinking, it is more often cocoa than vintage port. If ever the victory between town and gown has been decided, it has been decided now. And the victory is with Motopolis. Christminster is no longer a rival to the University, and the University is no longer a rival to Motopolis.

To escapists, to arty people like the author of these pages, the internal combustion engine is, next to wireless, the most sinister modern invention. It booms overhead with its cargo of bombs, it roars down the lanes with its cargo of cads, it poisons the air, endangers the streets, deafens the ears and deadens the senses. That its most successful manifestation in England should be at Oxford, of all places, passes belief.

Yet it is so, and the most arty of us must hand it to William Morris the Second. He has given employment to thousands, and money to millions; he has provided a cheap means of transport for hundreds of thousands. No doubt many persons injured by the engine he has helped to popularize have received the expert attention of the Oxford hospitals which he has so munificently endowed. It was only fitting that the University should honour him with a degree, and the country with a peerage.

Yet as the lanes of the country have become blue with the fumes of his success, so have the streets of this University life. And the streets are not only full of fumes. Other commercial enterprises have followed in the wake of the successful motor manufacturer. Speculative builders have run up strips of shoddy houses in almost every country lane around the town. East Oxford, where the works are, beyond Magdalen Bridge, is indistinguishable from Swindon, Neasden, or Tooting Bec. The architectural development of Oxford since the war has completely changed the character of the city.

The college buildings are endangered by motor traffic; main streets are as congested as the Strand; chain-stores have taken the place of small shopkeepers; small gas-lamps have given place to the great lamp-standards; buses have supplanted horse trams; the pale-faced mechanics in Oxford bags and tweed coats, walk down the Cornmarket; the farmers and labourers have disappeared; views are interrupted by motor-cars; open spaces occupied by car-parks; the commercial consistency in shop-front and sign of the last century has been ousted by the competitive garishness in imitation marble, electric light and lettering of big London-controlled enterprises. Oxford is no longer a provincial town. It is a replica of London.

The fate of Oxford has been the fate of most country towns. But there is no doubt that the Morris Motor Works have helped to make the transformation so rapid and complete. Cambridge, for instance, comparatively unblessed by industrialism, still retains its character.

William Morris the Second is not to be blamed for the ruination of Oxford. The fault lies almost entirely with the Colleges who allowed the land which they owned to become the muddled pretentiousness which passes today for a town.

In 1885 William Morris the First, poet, craftsman, Socialist, complained of the vulgarization of Oxford in *The Daily News*. He wrote on behalf of the old houses of the Christminster sort which were then numerous:

Oxford thirty years ago, when I first knew it, was full of these treasures; but Oxford 'culture', cynically contemptuous of the knowledge which it does not know, and steeped to the lips in the commercialism of today, has made a clean sweep of most of them; but those that are left are of infinite value, and still give some character above that of Victoria Street or Bayswater to modern Oxford.

But then he had little to complain of except of what his own Gothicizers were doing. Bayswater, certainly, and possibly Victoria Street, have more to be said for them than any of the post-war additions to Oxford. And North Oxford, which is, after all, only the brick and stone expression of the innate suburbanism of modern life, was for those days a neat and spacious bit of planning.

No, the fault lies with the colleges who for the last thirty years have been imbued with a parochialism which does not allow them to peep over their own mellow stone walls. It seems that their estate policy – and the colleges own vast estates from which their incomes are largely derived – has been influenced either by a desire to take no notice of the world outside Oxford, or else to make as much money out of it as is possible. There is, I suppose, no harm in the second policy so long as it is employed with foresight.

I have by me a *Whitaker's Almanack* for 1933, which gives the income of the Oxford Colleges.

Christ Church and Magdalen and, in a lesser degree, most of the other colleges of Oxford, were large landowners, according to *Kelly's Directory* for 1887, in just the districts which have been 'developed' in the most merciless way round Oxford since then ... You would suppose that Oxford University, the home of culture, the cluster of towers and spires whose fame has spread over five continents, whose portals are entered by reverent students from the older civilizations of the East – you would suppose this little Athens of European civilization, this cradle of toleration and enlightenment, would know something of the principles upon which a town is built.

Until one hundred years ago, the knowledge was still there. The colleges stood among their gardens, bounded by water on the south and east, and by Christminster on the west. To the north were farms. A little foresight, a little application of the innate aptitude for planning possessed by the eighteenth and early nineteenth centuries, would have preserved Oxford for ever.

They could have planned an industrial town, with all their learning, which would have been worthy of the University City beside it. The factories could have been planned away from the dwellings, the dwellings could have been set in green spaces and could have been handsome to look at. Morris Cowley could have been a model for the rest of England, so that visitors to the University, instead of trying to pretend no industrialism was near and bathing themselves in a false twilight of grey Gothic things, would have naturally hurried to see the living beauty of industrial Oxford after the dead glory of University architecture.

The colleges had it in their power to command good building. They could have been the chief landowners in the outskirts of the town. The material was there. The genius of William Morris the Second in motor manufacture could hardly have been expected to extend to town-planning. But there were all those books in the Bodleian, all those 'first-class brains' churning away in panelled senior common rooms.

You would have thought some concerted action had been possible. You would have imagined that architecture and town-planning had been heard of in the home of culture.

As it is, Oxford remains an unplanned muddle. Motopolis, Christminster and the University are jostled together in hopeless disorder. And if the Radcliffe Square still seems a quiet civic centre for the University, it is because no one has yet had the courage to take down the University Church and turn that desirable site into something more profitable than the alms-box in the South Porch.

An Approach to Oxford

The approaches to Oxford are the worst thing about it. None of them prepare you for a vision of the home of learning nestling grey among the elm surrounded meadows. I have made a mistake. There is *one* route, too circuitous and too laborious to be taken by any but the most romantic minded. You turn off the main road from High Wycombe just beyond Wheatley and make for Chipping Norton. After a few miles you branch left by shut-in lanes through grey Elsfield downhill to Marston. Here you take the footpath to Marston Ferry. At the ferry you board a punt or canoe or rob roy and paddle down the stream of the Cherwell to Magdalen Bridge.

The Cherwell is as romantic as it ever was – willows, meadows in which fritillaries have been found, a few boathouses and tea gardens with parents pouring out tea for self-conscious under-graduates. Under willows you will see punts moored close into the bank. The intellectual head of an undergraduette appears above the cushions, the pipe smoke of her admirer winds up among the leaves. A gramophone plays a dance tune. Gradually the subtle variations of a Bach fugue break in upon the dance. A punt rounds the corner, full of clever looking men in grey flannel trousers and shirt sleeves – sleeves of what shirts setting off what Czechoslovakian peasant-art ties! – this probably contains one of the younger dons with some promising pupils. Soon they will all be off on a reading party to the Pyrenees and when they return very few of them will be on speaking terms.

But let us not look into the future while we can see so much of the past.

As the shouts of the boys and the encouragement of the swimming instructors die away from the bathing place of the Dragon School behind us, the river takes a turn at a discreet female bathing place, and part of Oxford University is before us. We are in the University Parks where, of an afternoon, games are played on those dreary levels of sparse grass. In the distance Keble College pricks the skyline with its turrets and iron decorations. The river is spanned by an elegant concrete foot bridge, which humps itself like a Magpie Moth Caterpillar (*Abraxas grossulariata*). The effect is quite Japanese. This is the prettiest bridge for miles, a delicate piece of engineering unspoiled by 'architectural' additions.

Hoarse shouts, splashes, and screams sound above the thunder of a weir. We are at Parson's Pleasure, the open-air bathing place. There may be many parsons there, for all we can tell – clergymen are a great feature of North Oxford – but everyone is naked. Bodies lie stretched on the grass, looking up between the poplars, pipes jammed into mouths, sunlight dappling bald or long-haired heads.

We pull the boat over the rollers and the Cherwell winds on through the meadows of Mesopotamia to Magdalen Bridge. A gravel walk follows the river. Earnest students walk briskly along it, airing their brains before an evening's study. Snatches of conversation float down to us – 'Herodotus . . . first class mind . . . an alpha man . . . Aristotelian . . . Hegelian . . . Economic . . .' The conversation dies away. The river bends. The banks are steep and scooped away by the narrow stream. The trees of Addison's Walk hang over us. We are shut in by mud and grass. Somewhere about here it is, that you can hear the bells of Oxford better than from anywhere else. The sound sifted from the motor traffic carries across the meadows. I cannot particularize the bend in the stream without going in a boat to show you. It is some yards from Magdalen Bridge for the roar of the main road traffic is scarcely audible. Then you have to be spared the blaring of portable gramophones. But there *is* such a bend and no time is better to hear the bells than shortly before six on a still summer evening.

One – two, *One* – two, *One* – two. New College Tower is calling to choral evensong. Elsewhere college chapels and little high church places of worship where a lonely vicar will run through evensong to an old lady from North Oxford, keep up an insistent tinkle. Then Magdalen Tower breaks into a chime quite near, one two three four, four three two one, one two three four, four three two one. This sets the bells going all over the town. Finally the heavy boom from Tom Tower, Christ Church strikes the hours and puts an end to the dispute. Now the bells start for evening chapel at Magdalen, and somewhere a church tower, probably Carfax, strikes a belated six to defy the thunderings of Tom.

People have noticed these bells across the Oxford rivers for years. At the end of the eighteenth century, Cowper's friend, the Reverend James Hurdis, Professor of Poetry, thus remarked them:

> So have I stood at eve on Isis' banks,
> To hear the merry Christ-church bells ring round.
> So have I sat too in thy honoured shades
> Distinguish'd Magdalen, on Cherwell's brink,
> To hear thy silver Wolsey tones so sweet.
> And so too have I paus'd and held my oar
> And suffer'd the slow stream to bear me home,
> No speed required while Wykeham's peal was up.

With a bump we knock into the cluster of boats round Magdalen Bridge, thread our way through cushioned empty punts shaded by Magdalen Tower. So by willows, lovers, intellectuals, boys, bathers, bells, we have come right into the High Street of the University City; what more appropriate approach?

Blisland

Church crawling is the richest of pleasures, it leads you to the remotest and quietest country, it introduces you to the history of England in stone and wood and glass which is always truer than what you read in books. It was through looking at churches that I came to believe in the reason why churches were built and why, despite neglect and contempt, innovation and business bishops, they still survive and continue to grow and prosper, especially in our industrial towns.

Of all the country churches of the West I have seen I think the church of St Protus and St Hyacinth, Blisland, in Cornwall, is the most beautiful. I was a boy when I first saw it, thirty or more years ago. I shall never forget that first visit – bicycling to the inland and unvisited parts of Cornwall from my home by the sea. The trees at home were few and thin, sliced and leaning away from the fierce Atlantic gales, the walls of the high Cornish hedges were made of slate stuffed in between with fern and stone crop and the pulpy green triangles of mesembryanthemum, sea vegetation of a windy sea coast country. On a morning after a storm, blown yellow spume from Atlantic rollers would be trembling in the wind on inland fields. Then, as huge hill followed huge hill and I sweated as I pushed my bicycle up and heart-in-mouth went swirling down into the next valley, the hedges became higher, the lanes ran down ravines, the plants seemed lusher, the thin Cornish elms seemed bigger and the slate houses and slate hedges gave place to granite ones. I was on the edge of Bodmin Moor, that sweet brown home of Celtic saints, that haunted, thrilling land so full of ghosts of ancient peoples whose hut circles, beehive dwellings and burial mounds jut out above the ling and heather. Great wooded valleys, white below the trees with wood anemones or blue with bluebells, form a border fence on this, the western side of Bodmin Moor.

Perched on the hill above the woods stands Blisland village. It has not one ugly building in it and, which is unusual in Cornwall, the houses are round a green. Between the lichen-crusted trunks of elm and ash that grow on the green, you can see everywhere the beautiful moorland granite. It is used for windows, for chimney stacks, for walls. One old house has gable ends carved in it. They are sixteenth or seventeenth century and curl round like swiss rolls. The church is down a steep slope of graveyard, past slate headstones and it looks over the tree tops of a deep and elmy valley and away to the west where, like a silver shield, the Atlantic shines. An opening in the churchyard circle shows a fuchsia hedge and the Vicarage front door beyond. The tower is square and weathered and made of enormous blocks of this moorland granite, each block as big as a chest of drawers. When I first saw it, the tower was stuffed with moss and with plants which had rested here and there between the great stones. But lately it has been most vilely re-pointed in hard straight lines with cement. The church itself which seems to lean this way and that, throws out chapels and aisles in all directions. It hangs on the hillside, spotted with lichens which have even softened the slates of its roof. Granite forms the tracery of its windows, there is a granite holy-water stoup in the porch.

The whitewashed porch, the flapping notices, the door! That first thrill of turning the handle of the door of a church never seen before, or a church dearly loved and visited again and again like Blisland – who but the confirmed church crawler knows it?

Sir Ninian Comper, that great church architect, says that a church should bring you to your knees when first you enter it. Such a church is Blisland. For there before me as I open the door is the blue-grey granite arcade, that hardest of stones to carve. One column slopes outwards as though it was going to tumble down the hill and a carved wooden beam is fixed between it and the south wall to stop it falling. The floor is of blue slate and pale stone. Old carved benches of dark oak and a few chairs are the seating. The walls are white, the sun streams in through a clear west window and there – glory of glories! – right across the whole eastern end of the church is a richly-painted screen and rood loft. It is of wood. The panels at its base are red and green. Wooden columns, highly coloured and twisted like barley sugar, burst into gilded tracery and fountain out to hold a panelled loft. There are steps to reach this loft, in the wall. Our Lord and His Mother and St John who form the rood are over the centre of the screen. I look up and there is the old Cornish roof, shaped like the inside of an upturned ship, all its ribs richly carved, the carving shown up by white plaster panels. Old roofs, beautifully restored, are to be seen throughout the church. They stretch away beyond the cross irregularly and down the aisles. I venture in a little further, there through this rich screen I mark the blazing gold of the altars and the medieval-style glass, some of the earliest work of Mr Comper. In the nave is a pulpit shaped like a wineglass, in the Georgian style and encrusted with cherubs and fruit carved in wood.

The screen, the glory of the church, the golden altars, the stained glass and the pulpit are comparatively *new*, designed by F. C. Eden in 1897, who died a few years ago. He must have visualized this Cornish church as it was in medieval times. He did not do all the medieval things he might have done. He did not paint the walls with pictures of angels, saints and devils, he left the western windows clear that people might see their books; he put in a *Georgian* pulpit. He centred everything on the altar to which the screen is, as it were, a golden, red and green veil to the holiest mystery behind it.

What do dates and style matter in Blisland church? There is Norman work in it and there is fifteenth- and sixteenth-century work and there is sensitive and beautiful modern work. But chiefly it is a living church whose beauty makes you gasp, whose silent peace brings you to your knees, even if you kneel on the hard stone and slate of the floor, worn smooth by generations of worshippers.

The valley below the church was hot and warm when first I saw this granite cool interior. Valerian sprouted on the Vicarage wall. A fig tree traced its leaves against a western window. Grasshoppers and birds chirruped. St Protus and St Hyacinth, patron saints of Blisland church, pray for me! Often in a bus or train I call to mind your lovely church, the stillness of that Cornish valley and the first really beautiful work of man which my boyhood vividly remembers.

Bournemouth

Bournemouth is one of the few English towns one can safely call
'her'. With her head touching Christchurch and her toes turned
towards the Dorset port of Poole she lies, a stately Victorian duchess,
stretched along more than five miles of Hampshire coast. Her bed
has sand for under-blanket and gravel for mattress and it is as
uneven as a rough sea. What though this noble lady has lately dis-
figured her ample bosom with hideous pseudo-modern jewellery in
the shape of glittering hotels in the Tel-Aviv style, her handsome
form can stand such trashy adornment, for she is lovely still. Warm
breezes caress her. She is heavy with the scent of *Pinus laricio*, *Pinus
insignis*, the Scotch fir of orange-golden bark, the pinaster and black
Austrian pine. She wears a large and wealthy coat of precious firs.
Beneath it we may glimpse the flaming colours of her dress, the
winding lengths of crimson rhododendron, the delicate embroidery
of the flower beds of her numerous public gardens which change
their colours with the seasons. The blue veins of her body are the
asphalt paths meandering down her chines, among firs and sandy
cliffs, her life-blood is the young and old who frequent them, the
young running gaily up in beach shoes, the old wheeled steadily
down in invalid chairs. Her voice is the twang of the tennis racket
heard behind prunus in many a trim villa garden, the lap and roar of
waves upon her sand and shingle, the strains of stringed instruments
from the concert hall of her famous pavilion.

The sea is only one of the things about Bournemouth, and one of
the least interesting. Bathing is safe. Sands are firm and sprinkled
in places with shingle and in others with children. There are lines
of bathing huts, bungalows and tents and deck chairs municipally
owned, mostly above that long high water mark which hardly
changes at all, for the tide at Bournemouth always seems to be high.
Zig-zag paths, bordered by wind-slashed veronica, ascend those un-
spectacular slopes of sandy rock from Undercliffe to Overcliffe.
From Undercliffe the lazy motorist may shout out of her motor-car

window to her children on the beach, from Overcliffe she may survey the sweep of bay from Purbeck to the Needles, and, sickened by so much beauty, drink spirits in the sun lounge of one of those big hotels or blocks of flats which rise like polished teeth along the cliff top. The sea to Bournemouth is incidental, like the bathroom leading out of a grand hotel suite: something which is there because it ought to be, and used for hygienic reasons. Deep in a chine with its scent of resin and tap of palm leaves and plash of streamlets and moan of overhanging pine, an occasional whiff of ozone reminds us of the sea. But Bournemouth is mainly a residential town by the sea, not a seaside town full in summer only.

The inland suburbs of Bournemouth are like any other suburbs, indistinguishable from Wembley or the Great West Road. And they stretch for miles into Hants and Dorset, leaving here and there a barren patch of pylon-bisected heath. The main shopping streets have the usual ugly lengths of flashy chromium, though a pretty, early-Victorian stucco thoroughfare survives called the Arcade. The public buildings are less blatant and alien looking than the latest blocks of flats and hotels. But the beauty of Bournemouth consists in three things, her layout, her larger villas and her churches. All of these are Victorian.

Earliest Bournemouth is on the western and Branksome side of the Bourne which runs into the sea by the Pavilion. It consists of a few villas built by Mr Lewis Tregonwell whose name survives in a terrace and a road and whose house was part of the Exeter Hotel. He started building in 1810. In 1836 a local landlord, Sir George Tapps of Westover and Hinton Admiral, built on the eastern bank of the stream. Adding Gervis to his name, he went on building and called in Benjamin Ferrey, the Gothic church architect and friend of Pugin, to lay out his estate. Thus Gervis Place arose with its stucco Tudor-style villas. Tudor or Italian, the villas were varied, well spaced in their setting, roads were broad and planted with trees, but everything had to wind. Nothing was to be regular. That is why there is no formal promenade in Bournemouth and why there have always been so many footpaths and curving roads in the older and finer parts of the town. The place was carefully planned from its beginnings on the principle that nature abhors a straight line, the picturesque school of Georgian gardening surviving into Victorian times. This sense that Bournemouth is a garden with houses in it survived the century. The name Tapps-Gervis increased to Tapps-Gervis-Meyrick, hence Meyrick Avenue, Meyrick Park, Meyrick Road. And if you are not sure of the owner of the road, you may often guess its date from its name – Adelaide, Alma, Gladstone. They are hidden behind trees and flowering shrubs, down lengths of gravel bordered with rhododendron, these Victorian villas. Some are hotels, some are now government offices. They reflect every phase of leisured Victorian and Edwardian life – here a hint of Madeira, there an Elizabethan cottage, then an Italian villa like the Royal Bath Hotel. All these are in stucco and not later than the seventies. Then brick came in and we have 'Flemish style' buildings, with gables and white wood balconies and leaded panes, of which J. D. Sedding's Vicarage at St Clement's and big house at the top of Boscombe Chine, called The Knole, are beautiful, satisfying examples. They look stately and practical. Later, a brilliant local architect, Sidney Tugwell, designed villas in the new art style with tiny windows fluttering cheerful chintz, low-pitched roofs of local stone and broad eaves – wholesome and simple buildings like homemade cakes. He had his imitators. And each of these strongly individual Victorian houses, not content with its garden-like road, Knyveton Road, Manor Road, Alum Chine or further inland round Meyrick Park, has, or once had, a beautiful garden of its own. So that the real Bournemouth is all pines and pines and pines and flowering shrubs, lawns, begonias, azaleas, bird-song, dance tunes, the plung of the racket and creak of the basket chair.

Lastly the churches have the colour and clearness of the town. I doubt if any place in Britain has finer modern churches than Bournemouth and, what is more, they are all open and all alive. I visited fourteen of them on one week-day and found them all clean and cared for and in most of them people at prayer. Excluding Parkstone with its beautiful St Peter's and the lovely Basilica of St Osmund I thought the finest Bournemouth church was St Stephen's in the centre of the town – designed by J. L. Pearson. It is worth travelling 200 miles and being sick in the coach to have seen the inside of this many-vistaed church, all in clean cream-coloured stone, with arch cutting arch, a lofty hall of stone vaulting providing view after view as you walk round it, each lovelier than the next and worthy of a vast cathedral. Away in the suburbs there is much that is beautiful, J. D. Sedding's famous church of St Clement, scholarly and West-country looking in stone; Sir Giles Gilbert Scott's little Roman Catholic Church of the Annunciation, a brilliantly original design in brick, his first work after Liverpool Cathedral; St Francis' church by J. Harold Gibbons on a new building estate, white, Italianate and vast. As the day drew to an end I entered a red-brick church in a hard red-brick shopping street at the back of Boscombe. St Mary's, Boscombe, built about 1920. Here, out of the noise of the street, was a white, cool and spacious interior, friendly, beautiful, with golden screens and gold and blue east windows, gaily painted roofs and wide and high West-country arches. Clean and white and cheerful, the perfect seaside church. That last experience seemed to typify Bournemouth. You arrive tired from a long journey, you first see only the car parks, buses and jazzy blocks of flats and hotels. You turn into a side road and all is colour, light and life.

St Endellion

Saint Endellion! Saint Endellion! The name is like a ring of bells.
I travelled late one summer evening to Cornwall in a motor car.
The road was growing familiar, Delabole with its slate quarry
passed, then Pendogget. Gateways in the high fern-stuffed hedges
showed sudden glimpses of the sea. Port Isaac Bay with its sweep
of shadowy cliffs stretched all along to Tintagel. The wrinkled
Atlantic Ocean had the evening light upon it. The stone and granite
manor house of Tresungers with its tower and battlements was
tucked away out of the wind on the slope of a valley and there on the
top of the hill was the old church of St Endellion. It looked, and
still looks, just like a hare. The ears are the pinnacles of the tower
and the rest of the hare, the church, crouches among wind-slashed
firs.

On that evening the light bells with their sweet tone were being
rung for practice. There's a Ringer's rhyme in the tower, painted on
a board. It shows Georgian ringers in knee breeches and under-
neath is written a rhyme which ends with these fine four lines:

> Let's all in love and Friendship hither come
> Whilst the shrill treble calls to thundering Tom
> And since bells are for modest recreation
> Let's rise and ring and fall to admiration.

They were ringing rounds on all six bells. But as we drew near
the tower – a grand, granite, fifteenth-century tower looking across
half Cornwall – as we climbed the hill the bells sounded louder even
than the car. 'St Endellion! St Endellion!' they seemed to say.
'St Endellion' their music was scattered from the rough lichened
openings over foxgloves, over grey slate roofs, lonely farms and
feathery tamarisks, down to that cluster of whitewashed houses
known as Trelights, the only village in the parish, and to Roscarrock
and Trehaverock and Trefreock, heard perhaps, if the wind was
right, where lanes run steep and narrow to that ruined, forgotten

fishing place of Port Quin, 'St Endellion!'. It was a welcome to
Cornwall and in front of us the sun was setting over Gulland and
making the Atlantic at Polzeath and Pentire glow like a copper
shield.

Ora pro nobis Sancta Endelienta! The words are carved in strangely
effective lettering on two of the new oak benches in the church.
Incidentally, those carved benches, which incorporate some of the
old Tudor ones, are very decent-looking for modern pews. They
were designed by the present rector and carved by a local sculptress.
But who was St Endellion? She was a sixth-century Celtic saint,
daughter of a Welsh king, who with her sisters Minver and Teath
and many other holy relations came to North Cornwall with the
Gospel.

There was an Elizabethan writer who lived in the parish,
Nicholas Roscarrock. He loved the old religion and was imprisoned
in the Tower and put on the rack and then imprisoned again. He
wrote the life of his parish saint. 'St Endelient' he called her and
said she lived only on the milk of a cow:

which cowe the lord of Trenteny kild as she strayed into his grounds; and
as olde people speaking by tradition, doe report, she had a great man to
her godfather, which they also say was King Arthure, whoe took the
killing of the cowe in such sort, as he killed or caus'd the Man to be slaine,
whom she miraculously revived.

Nicholas Roscarrock also wrote a hymn in her praise:

> To emitate in part thy vertues rare
> Thy Faith, Hope, Charitie, thy humble mynde,
> Thy chasteness, meekness, and thy dyet spare
> And that which in this Worlde is hard to finde
> The love which thou to enemye didst showe
> Reviving him who sought thy overthrowe.

When she was dying Endelient asked her friends to lay her dead
body on a sledge and to bury her where certain young Scots bullocks
or calves of a year old should of their own accord draw her. This
they did and the Scots bullocks drew the body up to the windy
hilltop where the church now stands.

The churchyard is a forest of upright Delabole slate headstones, a rich grey-blue stone, inscribed with epitaphs – the art of engraving lettering on slate continued in this district into the present century – names and rhymes set out on the stone spaciously, letters delicate and beautiful. From the outside it's the usual Cornish church – a long low building of elvan stone, most of it built in Tudor times. But the tower is extra special. It is of huge blocks of granite brought, they say, from Lundy Island. The ground stage of the tower is strongly moulded but the builders seem to have grown tired and to have taken less trouble with the detail higher up, though the blocks of granite are still enormous.

I can remember Endellion before its present restoration. There's a photograph of what it used to look like in the porch – pitchpine pews, pitchpine pulpit, swamping with their yellow shine the clustered granite columns of the aisles. Be careful as you open the door not to fall over. Three steps *down* and there it is, long and wide and light and simple with no pitchpine anywhere except a lectern. A nave and two aisles with barrel roofs carved with bosses, some of them old but most of them done twelve years ago by a local joiner, the village postman and the sculptress. The floor is slate. The walls are stone lightly plastered blueish-grey. There is no stained glass. Old oak and new oak benches, strong and firm and simple, fill, but do not crowd, the church. They do not hide the full length of these granite columns. The high altar is long and vast. At the end of the south aisle is the sculptured base of St Endelienta's shrine, in a blue-black slate called Cataclewse, a boxwood among stones. The church reveals itself at once. Though at first glance it is unmysterious, its mystery grows. It is the mystery of satisfying proportion – and no, not just that, nor yet the feeling of age, for the present church is almost wholly early Tudor, not very old as churches go, nor is the loving use of local materials all to do with it. Why does St Endellion seem to go on praying when there is no one in it? The Blessed Sacrament is not reserved here, yet the building is alive.

There is something strange and exalting about this windy Cornish hill top looking over miles of distant cliffs, that cannot be put into words.

Down a path from the north door, bordered with fuchsias, is the

Rectory. The Rector of St Endellion is also a Prebendary. This church is run by a college of priests like St George's Chapel, Windsor. There are four prebends in the college, though their building is gone and they live elsewhere. They are the prebends of Marny, Trehaverock, Endellion and Bodmin. Each of the Prebendal stalls has a little income attached to it and is held by local priests. The money is given to Christian causes. For instance, the Parish of Port Isaac, formed out of St Endellion in 1913, is financed with the income of the Bodmin Prebendary. How this heavenly medieval arrangement of a college of prebendary clergymen survived the Reformation and Commonwealth and Victorian interferers is another mystery of St Endellion for which we must thank God. It was certainly saved from extinction by the late Athelstan Riley and Lord Clifden. Episcopal attacks have been made on it; but long live St Endellion, Trehaverock, Marny and Bodmin! Hold fast. *Sancta Endelienta, ora pro nobis!* ...

I take a last look at St Endellion standing on a cliff top of this Atlantic coast. The sun turns the water into moving green. In November weather, if the day is bright, the cliffs here are in shadow. The sun cannot rise high enough to strike them. The bracken is dead and brown, the grassy cliff tops vivid green; red berries glow in bushes. Ice cream cartons and cigarette packets left by summer visitors have been blown into crevices and soaked to pulp. The visitors are there for a season. Man's life on earth will last for seventy years perhaps. But this sea will go on swirling against these green and purple rocks for centuries. Long after we are dead it will rush up in waterfalls of whiteness that seem to hang half-way up the cliff face and then come pouring down with tons of ginger-beery foam. Yet compared with the age of these rocks, the sea's life is nothing. And even the age of rocks is nothing compared with the eternal life of man. And up there on the hill in St Endellion church, eternal man comes week by week in the Eucharist. That is the supreme mystery of all the mysteries of St Endellion.

Theo Marzials

Cast your mind back, if it will go back so far, to gaslight burning either side of the chimney piece; a large coal fire is leaping in the grate, fans and water colours are hung upon the walls, china is displayed on white enamel shelves rising tier above tier in one corner of the room. In another corner is a piano and beside it a silk screen – Louis Seize style. The folding doors of the sitting room have been thrown open into the dining room so as to make the place bigger. We are warm, well-fed and ready to be entertained. It is a suburban evening in the nineties and some friends have come in with their music. Mr and Mrs Pooter, Mr and Mrs Cummings, Gowing, Mr Padge, Eliza and her husband, and others. What harmonies we shall have, what arch looks will be cast between the palm leaves or above that vase of Cape gooseberries, and what are the songs that will be sung? I think it very likely that some of them will be by Theo Marzials, the most famous song-writer of the eighties and nineties. We shall have 'Twickenham Ferry'. Mr Pooter, will you sing that? It is suited to all tenor voices, and oh! the ripple of the air suggests the long lazy wave of brown Thames water down where the river is nearly tidal and rowing boats must take care.

[SONG: 'Twickenham Ferry']

And now that Mr Pooter has broken the ice, perhaps Carrie, his wife, will be brave enough to sing a duet with him – 'Go Pretty Rose'. I remember how well my father used to sing it in the bath.

[SONG: 'Go Pretty Rose']

And now what about one of the ladies on her own; this roguish little piece, since we are all warming up and enjoying ourselves – 'The Miller and the Maid'. I see that the words are by Mike Beverley and the music by Theo Marzials. But, as a matter of fact, Mike Beverley was a name Theo Marzials liked to assume when writing some of his lyrics – why, I have no idea.

[SONG: 'The Miller and the Maid']

And there is one piece of Marzials's which is still sung at school concerts and in village halls – 'Friendship'. The words really *are* by Sir Philip Sydney – Philip Sydney isn't another name for Marzials. The melody by Marzials is Elizabethan in flavour, for it was in Elizabethan lyrics and music that Marzials took the greatest delight. I expect that in somebody's drawing room, somebody listening to-night, there is a copy of that big, oblong book called *Pan-Pipes* with decorations by Walter Crane and music arranged by Marzials from Elizabethan and seventeenth-century lyrics. 1883, that was the date of the book. It looks like a stained glass window of that time as I open it before me.

[SONG: 'Friendship']

And now for the story of Marzials. Many years ago I went into a second-hand bookshop at the foot of Highgate Hill near Dick Whittington's stone and I bought for 1s. 6d. a book of poems called *The Gallery of Pigeons* by Theo Marzials. 1873 was the date but it was not the kind of poetry you would expect to read of that date. No, it was bold, strange, arty stuff, a foretaste of some of Swinburne's and William Morris's later work. Here are some character-istic lines that I remember:

> I chased her to a pippin-tree,
>   The waking birds all whist (*sic*),
> And oh! it was the sweetest kiss
>   That I have ever kiss'd.
>
> Marjorie (*sic*), mint, and violets
>   A-drying round us set,
> 'Twas all done in the faience-room
>   A-spicing marmalet;
> On one tile was a satyr,
>   On one a nymph at bay,
> Methinks the birds will scarce be home
>   To wake our wedding-day!

I imagine that last fantastic scene really means a room with William de Morgan tiles all round the walls and a table where some cherry-lipped maidens are putting spices into marmalade – a very daring fancy for 1873 or, indeed, for any age. Though I have quoted rather ridiculous lines of Marzials, he *was* a poet, there is no doubt about that. He was a stern critic of himself and I remember that my edition of his poems had comments which he had written in the margins – 'Naughty, naughty little Marzials', 'Pre-Lauberian period', 'Ridiculous, but I like it' and things like that. I started to look him up in books of reminiscences and I found tantalizing information. For instance, there was this by Ford Madox Hueffer in a book he wrote called *Ancient Lights*, published in 1911:

The mention of chocolate creams reminds me of another musician who was also a Pre-Raphaelite poet – Mr Theo Marzials. Mr Marzials was in his young days the handsomest, the wittiest, the most brilliant and the most charming of poets. He had a career tragic in the extreme and, as I believe, is now dead. But he shared with M the habit of keeping chocolate creams loose in his pocket, and on the last occasion when I happened to catch sight of him looking into a case of stuffed birds at South Kensington Museum, he had eaten five large chocolates in the space of two minutes.

Hueffer admired Marzials's poems and quotes one of his little tragedies in two verses:

> She was only a woman, famish'd for loving,
>   Mad with devotion, and such slight things;
> And he was a very great musician,
>   And used to finger his fiddle-strings.

> Her heart's sweet gamut is cracking and breaking
>   For a look, for a touch, – for such slight things;
> But he's such a very great musician,
>   Grimacing and fing'ring his fiddle-strings.

Then I remember in a book of reminiscences by H. de Vere Stacpoole – there were some references to Marzials's genius and to his having been led astray in Paris.

Then came the great time when I spent a whole day with Max Beerbohm and I asked him about Marzials. 'Theo Marzials,' he said, 'oh yes, wasn't he rediscovered by Henry Harland?' – *re*discovered, mark you, so he must have been well-known as a poet and musician before the days of Wilde and the Yellow Book – 'And didn't he take stimulants in order to shine at Aubrey Beardsley's parties?' And then he told me how Marzials had been in the British Museum library as a clerk at the same time as Edmund Gosse when the great Panizzi, the librarian who founded the British Museum Reading Room, was in command there. Marzials was always a highly picturesque figure with flowing moustaches, long hair and a silk tie which fell in folds over the lapels of his coat. When out of doors he wore a wide-awake hat. He must indeed have been a picturesque figure in the British Museum Reading Room while Karl Marx was scratching away at *Das Kapital* and various mad antiquarians were hiding among pyramids of books. Anyhow, one day Marzials was in the gallery of that enormous, silent Reading Room – and if you have not seen it you can imagine it as something like the dome of St Paul's – when the great Panizzi came in. Suddenly, Marzials leant over the gallery and, in a loud voice, said 'Am I or am I not the darling of the Reading Room?'

With these tit-bits of information I went to see my friend Martin Secker, the publisher, who knows more about the nineties than most people, and he was so interested that he put a letter in the *Sunday Times* asking for information about Marzials, poet and eccentric. He had some fascinating replies. To begin with, Marzials was not dead in 1911 as a result of drink and drugs in Paris. No. He had spent most of the time in the West of England living first in Blandford, Dorset, and then with his sister in Colyton, Devon. She predeceased him by many years and he died in 1920 at Mrs Power's farm of Elm Grove, Colyton. He was aged seventy. I wondered how he had gone on all those years between when he was a famous singer and poet, the flashing centre of Bohemian parties and drawing-room concerts, and those last years when he was living outside a tiny Devonshire town as a paying guest in a farmhouse.

Mr Zealley, who had been a boy at Colyton when Marzials was an old man there, has allowed me to take this extract from his letter:

He lived quite alone, and it is certainly true that he was a most eccentric and striking figure in the rural community in which he lived. His interest in music was the outstanding feature which made him known to the villagers. He attended all concerts that were held, and almost inevitably caused consternation by standing up in the audience and declaiming, in his very strong accent, most outspoken, not to say rude, criticisms of the efforts of the performers. This was particularly the case if he thought he detected any form of affectation or musical insincerity. I remember on one occasion a lady, who really sang quite well, and who had a great affection for Italy in which she travelled a great deal, singing a song to a village audience in Italian and in the operatic style of that country. Brushing aside (not without physical violence) all efforts to dissuade him, Marzials got himself on the platform and sang 'Madam will you walk?' in the Italian manner, with every sort of trill and musical exaggeration.

The most interesting letter of all comes from Mr F. G. Skinner who had known him well in his declining years. Really, I must read you nearly all of it. Mr Skinner stayed with Marzials at Elm Grove farmhouse and says:

Theo had one fair-sized room on the ground floor with a single bed in one corner, occupying it day and night. By his bedside was a small table on which there always seemed to be a saucer containing sliced beetroot in vinegar so that the room continually smelt of this, together with the odour of chlorodyne (which he took to induce sleep), with, at night, the fumes of an enormous oil-lamp. During conversation, he would often fish out a slice of beetroot on the end of a fork and drop it into his mouth most elegantly – it was almost a joy to watch him. In another corner of the room, he kept a huge stockpot on a stove, into which he threw all sorts of odds and ends so that he had a kind of perpetual stew. What he did with it I do not know, but we thought he gave it to some of the poorer farm-hands elsewhere.

As to his appearance, he was certainly the most striking figure I have met, fairly tall and of huge girth. When he sat down at the piano he dominated it by his size as well as by his genius. His hair was snow-white, his complexion as pink and clear as a healthy child's and although his clothes were odd and often the worse for wear, his person was always very well groomed. When I used to call and ask him to come out for a drink, he would slide out of bed, put on a tie, boots with no laces, no socks (he seldom wore socks) and join me with gusto. He seemed to love it. If we went to certain pubs he would go in with me to the bar-parlour and drink a pint or two of old-and-mild: but once I suggested going into the Colcombe Castle Hotel and he said 'All right' but made me go into the Lounge while he went into the public bar with the locals, I passing his beer through a kind of hatchway. He said he wasn't dressed for the

Saloon Lounge – and he was the most important man in my mind for miles around!

He often seemed to have no money and would occasionally beg me, as I was a Christian, to give him sixpence or a shilling. I knew that he went later to the confectioners and bought lollipops for the village children. I believe that his income was sent direct to his landlady and that most of it went for board and lodging so that very little was left for pocket money.

He used to go mostly to Ye Olde Bear Inn, where I often stayed, and where in an upper room he would play and sing, even when nearly seventy, in a fine, rich, deep baritone – oh! splendid, splendid. His speaking voice, too, was a delight to hear – magnificently rich, and when he was roused in any way it was like thunder.

While speaking of his voice, I must mention another habit. He was sometimes seen and heard walking barefooted in the garden of Elm Grove in the small hours – one or two o'clock in the morning. He would sing in a very soft, low voice and now and then take a flower between his fingers, bend down and kiss it, and murmur 'O my pretty!' Theo Marzials – poet and eccentric!

He was ravenous for reading matter and annotated the books I used to send him with many interesting scribblings. Here is a sample – written under a picture of George Meredith:

'He was audience to my first singing of "Summer Shower". Mrs M. (No. 2) a tall, dignified, comely, sympathetic French woman, loving and by G. M. most beloved, used to be most kind about my speciality of French very old songs. I first met her at Mendelssohn's cousin's (Box Hill). I was the hired singer – 25 gns. for 3 songs – a lot in the 70's.'

I remember that sometimes after a long evening at Ye Olde Bear I would walk back to Elm Grove with Theo. He insisted on taking my arm – no easy thing for me as I weighed only eight stone while he must have turned fifteen stone – and although I could have walked the distance in three minutes, it generally took us twenty minutes or half an hour. He would keep on stopping and talking – books, music, art, local gossip, anything.

One conversation has always lingered with me. I started it by asking him whether he had seen that Mr Alfred Noyes had written that he (Noyes) considered the finest single line in English poetry to be Shakespeare's

Following darkness like a dream.

That was enough to keep us up till about two in the morning, with Theo quoting, quoting from Chaucer to Newbolt. He had a marvellous memory and could roll off passage after passage with ease and splendour. But what I most remember is that when I rose to go to bed that night, he put his hand on my shoulder and said, 'Well, Fred, my boy, you can take it or leave it, but as far as my judgement is worth anything, *I* say that the finest single *verse* in English poetry, Shakespeare, Milton and all the rest of 'em included, is Mrs Alexander's

> There is a green hill far away,
> Without a city wall,
> Where our dear Lord was crucified
> Who died to save us all.

Theophile Jules Henri Marzials – poet, and *not* so eccentric perhaps, after all!

The last person who wrote to us, and whom I must mention, is Mrs Belt. She is the daughter of Cyril Davenport, the great friend of Marzials's youth who drew the picture of him in a wide-awake hat which I mentioned earlier. This letter from Marzials to Mrs Belt is very touching. It was written from Colyton in 1918, two years before his death and when he had had a stroke which had paralysed him down one side:

. . . I kept my voice almost intact until this last 'breaking up.' But who cares to hear an old man sing? This is a rambling Dairy-farm. Folk come in summer and take rooms and some used to pay-guest or board, but since the war and rations &c. they don't. It is all very clean. The head is a wonderful old woman and she and I live here. She in her part and I in mine. I sup with them. The niece housekeeps. Her husband does for me – and in his way is very like Cyril and me – in fact it is very like the situation of when your mama and papa and me were all just married, as it were. Of the folk who come and go in the house, I don't often mix up with them. Cyril knows my fits of retirement and since all this dying and the war I make no new friends – oh, I couldn't. Cyril is a bit of me – of course, and always was and ever will be. We just meet and are side by side, arm in arm, heart to heart, as if he had gone into a shop and I was waiting outside. Dear old Squirrel. This is a most beautiful place, of endless and immediate variety. I have never known a place like it, in this respect. Seaton is the ugliest sea-side I have ever seen, too commonplace to be odious – but the seventeen odd miles of wildlandslip just off Seaton is quite perfection – and quite undescribable. And your wonderful letter. And oh what a gentle-woman you must be . . .

On a lovely day in the spring of this year, I went to Colyton to find Marzials's grave. I had never been to this unspoiled and beautiful little Devonshire town before. It is a huddle of cream and pink washed thatched cottages collected round a silver-grey church tower and it lies in a little lush Devonshire valley with small hills around it. The cemetery is high above the town and looks down towards the farm where Marzials lived, over a landscape, as he describes it, 'of endless and immediate variety'. There was the grave with his sister's name above and his own below on a stone cross –

'Theophile Jules Henri Marzials. Born at Bagnères de Bigorre, Hautes-Pyrénées, France, December 20th, 1850. Died at Colyton, February 2nd, 1920. Fight the Good Fight of Faith.'

Let us go back to that evening party where we started. The refreshments are over and only one more song is to be sung. Let it be that most famous of all his songs and lyrics 'The River of Years' – once sung by throaty tenors at village concerts and evening parties all over the English-speaking world, and even joked about in *Punch* by Phil May. And as we listen – if it isn't too inappropriate at a party – let us remember him whose body has been lying so long forgotten in that Devonshire hillside and whose soul is, I pray, in that fair daylight of his song.

[SONG: 'The River of Years']

The Isle of Man

Not long ago I stepped out of an Edwardian electric tram-car on to the grassy height of Snaefell, two thousand feet above sea-level. The day was clear and I could see Snowdon seventy-three miles away to the south-west and, much nearer, the mountains of Cumberland, the Mull of Galloway and, in the west, the mountains of Mourne – four countries in bluish outline beneath a sky of mother-of-pearl and a wrinkled sea all round us, cloud-patched with streaks of purple.

Four countries seen from a fifth – this ancient kingdom of Man which once owned the Sodor or southern islands of Scotland. The tram-car returned down the mountainside. Many who had landed at the top went into the café for tea or beer and I had, for a moment, the whole island to myself, thirty-two miles long and twelve wide at my feet; brown moorland and mountain in the middle with tiny fields on the lower slopes, green slate and blue slate, silver lime-stone and red sandstone, gorse and blaeberries and ling, gigantic cliffs and hidden, wooded glens, foxgloves, fern and scabious on Cornish-looking hedges, whitewashed cottages thatched with straw and drowned in fuchsia bushes. It is a bit of Ulster set down in the sea, a bit of England, Scotland, Wales and Cornwall too, a place as ancient as them all, a separate country, Norse and Celtic at once.

The Isle of Man, like Shakespeare, has something memorable for everyone. It is a place of strong contrasts and great variety. Yet in southern England it is hardly known at all.

Yet from June to September half a million people cross from the coast of Lancashire, whole towns at a time. Then lodging houses are stuffed to capacity, then bathing things hang from the sixth floor downwards, then the main road round the island, the famous T.T. track, hums with 'charas', and still there is room. Each time I have visited the Isle of Man it has been at the height of the season and each time I have been able to lose myself in the country. I have tramped knee-deep in blaeberry bushes on the wild west coast of the island, looking in vain for the ruins of a Celtic chapel and never seeing a soul till I turned inland and walked down rutty farm lanes between foxgloves and knapweed to the narrow-gauge railway. And on the same evening I have been able to lose myself again in the crowds on Douglas front, to see Norman Evans in variety at the Palace and afterwards to watch a thousand couples dance in one of the big halls. All this in so small a kingdom, such wildness and such sophistication, such oldness and such newness. The trams, the farms, the switchback railways, the mountain sheep, the fairy lights and the wood-smoke curing kippers – how can I cram them all in? The clearest way of describing the island is to divide it into the two peoples of which it consists, the Manx and the visitors.

And the Manx come first. When the last boat of holiday-makers has steamed out of Douglas harbour back to Lancashire, about fifty thousand Manx are left behind: the Christians, Quayles, Crellins, Kewleys, Caines, Kermodes, Clucases, Kellys, Cregeens – Manx names seem almost all to begin with C, K or Q. They are a shy, poetical people. The look of their country is Celtic. There are small-holdings and plenty of *antiquities*, but not much ancient architecture. The island looks like Cornwall, Wales and Ireland mixed. But Man is Norse as well as Celtic. Until 1266 it belonged to Norway. Race enthusiasts see in the long, tall Manxmen with their fair hair and blue eyes and long moustaches, the descendants of the Vikings. Man was the capital of a Viking kingdom of islands, and very well the Vikings ran it and very slowly they adopted the Christian religion of the conquered Celts. Then the Scots took it over and finally Edward III, the strong man of the time, made England overlord. In 1405 Henry IV gave it to the Stanley family. The Stanleys became not only Earls of Derby but Kings of Man. And when that line of Stanleys died out, the kingship passed to a descendant, the Duke of Atholl. Late in the eighteenth century Man was still an independent country, an unknown island of mists and cliffs and smugglers with a king who was usually non-resident. Spain and France and Portugal shipped dutiable goods to Douglas and Castle-town and other Manx ports. Manx sailors would run specially de-signed fast ships to England. By their own laws they were doing nothing illegal. They were only breaking British laws.

The island was also a place of refuge for debtors at this time when, by the laws of England and Ireland, a person could still be imprisoned for debt. I believe that Sir William Hillary, founder of the National Lifeboat Institution, who lived at Falcon Cliff, Douglas, was one of these debtors, though he did nothing but good to the Isle of Man. On the other side of Douglas Bay the ruined rake 'Buck Whaley' built himself Fort Anne, now an hotel, where, safe from his creditors, he wrote his memoirs. He died in 1800.

Assuming much moral indignation about the smugglers and debtors who had settled on Man, as well as seeing that the island might be both profitable financially and useful in times of war, the British Government bought out the last claims of the Duke of Atholl to kingship of Man in 1828 for nearly half a million pounds. This was an immense sum for the period, but the British Government gained in the long run. The only people who did not do well out of this sale were the Manx.

He who has not seen the Tynwald on Tynwald Day does not know how ancient and independent Man is. Of course the feel of another country is in the air as soon as one lands. It is an island, it has generous licensing hours, it has its own flag of three armoured legs on a red background, its own language (half Scottish, half Northern-Irish Gaelic), its own customs in both senses of that word. But the full Manxness shines on 5 July, the annual holiday of Tynwald Day. The centre of the island is St John's. Here most valleys meet and here surrounding mountains hide the sea. Carts from all the sheadings, tall men from Rushen in the south, small men from the white fuchsia-hidden farms of Ayre in the north, from forgotten holdings deep in the primeval forests of the Curraghs, from cottages in sycamore-shaded glens, from lonely houses on the sides of mountains, and from the narrow lanes of Peel that smell of wood-smoke and kippers, from the stately old capital of Castletown with its silver limestone castle, from the noble Welch Gothic range of King William's College, from Ramsey with its delicate Georgian Court House, from Douglas, that Naples of the North, from forgotten hamlets like Ronague on the slopes of South Barrule, from the stricken terraces by deserted lead-mines of Foxdale, from Laxey where the greatest water-wheel in the world stands idle for ever, and from the sheltered lanes of Port St Mary, the Manxmen come to Tynwald fair. The little railway runs extra trains. All sorts of extraordinary rolling stock, made in the nineties and as good as ever, is drawn by little engines past creamy meadowsweet and brown mountain streams to the curious junction of St John's. And there not far from the station is Tynwald Hill itself, an artificial mound of grass, eighty feet high with four circular terraces around it.

On 5 July, a cream canopy tops the mound to shelter the Governor of Man who will represent the King, and down the straight avenue that leads to the church white masts fly alternately the flags of Britain and of Man. St John's Chapel is a golden granite spired building in that dashing and original style of romantic Gothic invented by John Welch which characterizes almost all Manx established churches and which is Georgian in origin, though often Victorian in execution. The path to the church is strewn with rushes, offerings to a pagan sea god older than the Viking Tynwald mound. As eleven strikes, the sun streams down, a hymn from A. and M. is relayed from the church; the chief people in the island are assembled for public worship. The Coroners, the Captains of the Parishes, the Clergy in their robes, the Chairmen of the Town Commissioners of Peel, Ramsey and Castletown in frock coats, the Mayor of Douglas all in red and ermine; they step out into the sunlight from the west door. And so do the Vicar-General, the Archdeacon, the High Bailiff – all these legal-clerical-looking men – the Members of the House of Keys, their Chaplain and their Speaker, the Government Secretary, the Members of the Legislative Council, the Attorney-General, the two Deemsters in their robes of red who are the judges of the island, and the Lord Bishop of Sodor and Man – that luckless Bishop whose cathedral is a beautiful ruin of green slate and red sandstone on an islet overlooking Peel, that luckless Bishop who has a seat in the English House of Lords but no vote in it – who is second in command of the island. And now comes the Sword of State, a thirteenth-century Scandinavian relic, and behind it the Lieutenant-Governor himself with a posse of police and the Surgeon to the Household keeping up the rear. Slowly they ascend to Tynwald Hill, the Governor to the top and the rest in order of importance on terraces below. The Coroner fences the court. Then the Deemster reads out the latest laws in English and a priest reads them out again in Manx. It is all beautifully organized and it goes on for a long time. But here in this ancient circle of the hills time seems nothing. As the old Manx language is read out, the sun shines down on us, although the peaks of every mountain round us are hidden in clouds. It is always fine, I am told, at St John's on Tynwald Day. The magician who lived in the island up to the fifth century used to make a mist to hide the island from its invaders, and it is certainly true that whenever Man has been visited by English king or queen it has been shrouded in mist, even at a recent visit of King George VI.

Fishing and farming were once the chief industries of the Manx. Fishing has dwindled so that there are now only nine boats Manx-manned and owned among all the little drifters that set out into the evening for herrings. The other hundred are mostly Scottish. And even farming takes second place to the greatest Manx industry, which is catering.

This brings me to the most enjoyable thing in all the enjoyment of Man – the visitors. I wish I knew when it was that these mass migrations from Lancashire started. Perhaps I can tell most easily from looking at Douglas. If I stand on Douglas Head and look across that noble sweep to Onchan Head, before the fairy lights are on and while the sun setting behind the mountains still lets me see the out-line of the houses on the front, I can trace the recent history of the island.

The original Douglas at my feet, around the harbour, is a small fishing port, not half so beautiful as Castletown further down this eastern coast – Castletown with its magnificent medieval-moated and turreted castle, its box-pewed, three-deckered, still unspoilt church, its exciting stone police station by Baillie Scott, and its Doric column to Governor Smelt. What made Douglas grow was its natural scenery, but people did not notice natural scenery until Georgian times. The last Duke of Atholl to be governor had the Shrewsbury architect George Stewart design him, in 1804, a palace on this noble sweep of bay. It is known today in its smooth, silvery stone as Castle Mona Hotel. Its dining-room is the finest room on the island, the Adam style at its simplest and most graceful. Only that exquisite country house the Nunnery, in Walter Scott Gothic by John Pinch, compares with it. And after the Duke, the debtors escaping to Mona with some cash, and other visitors, built themselves romantic castles on these heights above the bay – Falcon Cliff, Fort Anne, Derby Castle. These are late Georgian castellated buildings designed to look like romantic ruins by John Welch who also built in 1832 the Tower of Refuge on a rock in the middle of the water in Douglas Bay and so turned a looming danger into the semblance of an ancient castle. Then in the reign of William IV the gaps between the castles were filled in with stately stucco terraces, Brighton fashion (Windsor Terrace and Mount Pleasant are the best) sometimes high on the cliffs and here and there on the sea shore. The effect was and is magically beautiful. These Georgian terraces and Walter Scott, Peveril-of-the-Peak style castles flash out upon the cliff side. But this exclusive and romantic watering place cannot originally have been designed for half a million north-country folk – more likely for a few hundred half-pay officers eking out their pensions here where taxes are low.

I think the man of genius who turned the island into what it is, and saved it from ruin so that it is now financially prosperous, was Governor Loch. He improved the harbours and built the Loch Promenade in the sixties and seventies. Thereafter Douglas-style boarding-houses appeared in rows wherever there were gaps between the old terraces. They are innocent enough five-storeyed, bay-windowed, gabled buildings, gloomy behind, sea-gazing in front, rows and rows and rows of them so that the distant effect is of white paper folded into a concertina and perched here and there and everywhere along the shore. They are not as disfiguring as the modern bungalows and clumsily arranged electric light poles which ruin so much of the country part of Man. And now what with the T.T., the motor races, the improved harbours, the way everybody is out to be gay, *however* gloomy you are feeling you cannot be ill-humoured in Douglas. The boats arrive, the aeroplanes come down, young men and old in open shirts, sports coats and grey flannels, young girls and old in cheerful summer dresses, queue for ices, queue for shrimps, crowd round bars for glasses of delicious dry champagne, gaze from horse-trams over municipal flowerbeds to the

Tower of Refuge and the sea, travel in luxury coaches round the
island half asleep in one another's arms till the sun sets behind the
boarding-houses of Douglas and all the lights go up and the dance
halls begin to fill. It is nine o'clock. There is still light in the sky.
Father and mother, basking in one another's love, are sitting in
chairs on the steps of the boarding-house; behind the front door
peeps the inevitable castor oil plant in its china pot. Beside them
sit the younger children, unnaturally good and quiet for fear they
shall be sent up to bed while it is still light and while the moon rises
huge and yellow above the purple bay. The elder children, grown
up now, are off to the dance halls. Only a few rejected young men
sit sadly on the steps among the ancients and the infants. The girls
wear white dancing shoes and that is how you know whither they
are bound. Two shillings or four-and-six, somewhere round that, is
the cost of a ticket to dance. I like the Palace dance hall best. It has
a parquet floor of sixteen thousand square feet and room for five
thousand people. It is in a gay baroque style, cream and pink inside,
and from the graceful roof hang Japanese lanterns out of a dangling
forest of flags. A small and perfect dance band strikes up – ah, the
dance bands of the Isle of Man! Soon a thousand couples are mov-
ing beautifully, the cotton dresses of the girls like vivid tulips in all
this pale cream and pink, the sports coats and dark suits of the men
a background to so much airy colour. The rhythmic dance is almost
tribal, so that even a middle-aged spectator like me is caught up in
mass excitement, pure and thrilling and profound.

And while the dance bands are playing in Douglas and the yellow
moon is rising in its bay, on the western, wilder coast the herring
fleet is setting out from Peel. The sun sets behind the rugged out-
line of the Castle and the ruined Cathedral and Round Tower en-
closed within its walls. A stiffish west wind is blowing and the sea
beyond the breakwater is dark green and choppy. The herring boats
are disappearing into the sunset. Out of the harbour, round the
castle island, the dying sun shines gold upon their polished sides. I
stand alone upon a rock by Peel Castle. The smell of salt and wet
earth is in my nostrils, the dark green slate of those old castle walls
is at my side. Inland, the last rays of sun are lighting the winding
lanes of Peel, the red sandstone of its church towers, and the soft

protecting mountains behind it of the Isle of Man. Here, salt spray, seagulls, wild rocks and cavernous cliffs. Beyond those mountains the dance halls of Douglas and the dance-band leader in his faultless tails. An isle of contrasts! A miniature of all the Western world.

Kelmscott

The best way of all to approach Kelmscott is the way William Morris, the poet, craftsman and Socialist, used to come to this house of his dreams – by the river. Kelmscott Manor House is on the banks of the upper Thames. It's not the sort of Thames of Boulter's Lock and Maidenhead night-clubs, not those used and wide waters, but a Thames that is almost a stream up between the last locks. There are more kingfishers than boats, and many dragon-flies like gleaming aeroplanes, and meadowsweet and willows and irises, and flat, almost Lincolnshire landscape on the Oxfordshire bank where Kelmscott stands. The roads round here are like streams themselves, winding among unfenced or low hedged fields, past greyish-golden cottages of stone, and barns and dovecots and little churches. It is all like England was in the sixteenth century when the Turners first built themselves this gabled manor house. Their descendants, the Hobbes family, still farm most of the land round it.

Now here is William Morris coming to the house as he describes it in *News from Nowhere*:

Over the meadow I could see the mingled gables of a building where I knew the lock must be, and which now seemed to combine a mill with it. A low wooded ridge bounded the river-plain to the south and south-east, whence we had come, and a few low houses lay about its feet and up its slope. I turned a little to my right, and through the hawthorn sprays and long shoots of the wild roses I could see the flat country spreading out far away under the sun of the calm evening, till something that might be called hills with a look of sheep-pastures about them bounded it with a soft blue line. Before me, the elm-boughs still hid most of what houses there might be in this river-side dwelling of men; but to the right of the cart-road a few grey buildings of the simplest kind showed here and there ... We crossed the road, and again almost without my will my hand raised the latch of a door in the wall, and we stood presently on a stone path which led up to the old house.

Before we go in, let us walk round this grey stone walled garden among the box borders, the cut yews and the roses. It's not a very big house, and I think that why anybody likes it so much is because it is small and something they feel they could live in and love themselves. If you weren't sure, you would say this old stone house – purple when wet with rain, gold in sunlight when seen against dark green trees or approaching storm clouds – if you weren't sure, and like me, you were someone who thought he knew about architecture, you would say it was mostly Tudor. But I believe it is later – more like Charles I's time; for the tradition of stone masonry lingered on in this remote place even until well into the last century. And you will notice that one wing on the north is grander than the rest of the house with carvings on the outside which are a hundred years later than Tudor. And while we are outside, look at the farm buildings: barns as big as churches all in the local stone, and high stone walls. They all seem to have grown with the landscape. 'If you touched them,' Janey Morris said to Rossetti, 'you would expect them to be alive.'

The house inside is very much as it was except that electric light has been introduced, there are water closets, and two bathrooms with immersion heaters. As Morris said, 'Everywhere there was but little furniture, and that only the most necessary, and of the simplest forms.' And I must say that today, you could not say Kelmscott was disappointing inside. The furniture is solid stuff, some of it heavily hand-made and painted by Morris and Rossetti. And some of it is Elizabethan. There is a great four-poster Elizabethan bed in which William Morris used to sleep – an inconvenient place, and not a very comfortable bed either. Anyone going into the tapestry room had to make their way past him lying in his bed. Round the posts at the top of the bed is a border with words embroidered by May Morris. It begins like this:

> The wind's on the wold
> And the night is a-cold,
> And Thames runs chill
> Twixt mead and hill
> But kind and dear
> Is the old house here

> And my heart is warm
> Midst winter's harm.

The ornaments in the house are mostly blue pottery, collected I believe by Rossetti. There are drawings of Mrs William Morris by Rossetti – Janey Morris with her long, long neck and chin, her full lips and sleepy eyes and flaming hair, who was so adored by Rossetti from the days he first met her at Oxford when he and Morris and others were painting the roof of the Library of the Oxford Union. I suppose the grandest room is the drawing-room with its white Georgian panelling on the ground floor in that north wing of the house I described when we were outside. And about equally grand is the tapestry room above it – though I could, like Rossetti, do without the tapestry which has been there since the seventeenth century. It depicts the life of Samson, and one particularly gruesome scene shews Samson having his eyes gouged out. The rooms I like best are the older ones at the west end; the ground floor room which Rossetti moved into for a studio when he painted Janey Morris. His palette and paints are still there. Above it is a bedroom all papered in that green willowy pattern paper Morris designed which is so like the willowy lanes round here, and seems to be made almost of living branches. Throughout the house there are Morris papers, and Morris chintzes – the Strawberry Thief, the Daisy, and so on – flowered chintzes and papers which make it seem as though the beautiful garden outside had walked into the house and stylized itself on the walls and chairs and curtains.

I have not bothered you with a detailed tour of this rambling little manor house. What you cannot fail to notice and what is worth mentioning last and emphasizing most, is its atmosphere. It haunts one. I know of no house with so strong an atmosphere. There is no other place which is kept as it was and yet so clearly is not a museum but a home. Come up to the first floor and look out of one of the windows over the tops of the yews and the flowering trees, through the great elms and into the wide upper Thames meadows. Winter and summer for three centuries while the Turner family lived here this stone grew lichened and from those water spouts the heavy rain fell on to the deep green grass of the garden from between the gables. Never did you hear such a noise of English wet as when the rain pours off Kelmscott Manor roof and splashes on to the grass and garden paths! And sometimes the Thames would rise and flood the garden.

Yet I think the chief atmosphere here is of those Pre-Raphaelite tenants, William Morris and Dante Gabriel Rossetti. Rossetti, in love with Mrs Morris, remained at Kelmscott, getting more and more moody, imagining plots against him, staying awake till five in the morning, taking chloral, and only going out when he would meet few villagers. But he had his moments of loving the place, and since he was in love, he produced some fine poems.

In 1877 Rossetti left Kelmscott never to return. Thereafter Morris came back, but used it chiefly as a country retreat, a holiday house for his wife and children, while he remained in London at his Hammersmith house which he also called Kelmscott House after his country manor. There in Hammersmith he did his printing and made his Socialist speeches and tore bits out of his black beard when he grew angry.

I like to think of him in a summer of 1880 setting out with three near friends and his wife to row from Kelmscott, Hammersmith, to Kelmscott, Oxon. The boat looked like a horse bus on water with a pair of oars in the prow. They reached Oxford after seven days:

... Janey the next day (Monday) went on by rail to Kelmscott: while we got up early and by dint of great exertions started from Medley Lock at 9 a.m., with Bossom and another man to tow us as far as New Bridge, where we sent them off, and muddled ourselves home somehow, dining at a lovely place about a mile above New Bridge, where I have stopped twice before for that end. One thing was very pleasant: they were hay-making on the flat flood-washed spits of ground and islets all about Tadpole; and the hay was gathered on punts and the like; odd stuff to look at, mostly sedge, but they told us it was the best stuff for milk ... Charles was waiting for us with a lantern at our bridge by the corner at 10 p.m., and presently the ancient house had me in its arms again: J. had lighted up all brilliantly, and sweet it all looked you may be sure ...

Sixteen years later in the early autumn of 1896 William Morris died. His body was carried to the little churchyard from Kelmscott Manor House in a yellow farm waggon with red wheels, wreathed with vine and willow boughs.

My own happiest memories of Kelmscott date from as late as the thirties, when May, Morris's surviving daughter, and her friend Miss Lobb lived in the Manor House. My wife and I used to drive there by pony cart and were always welcomed with a huge tea and a feed for the pony, for May Morris loved anything that was not to do with this mechanized age. She used to show us the beautiful vellum books her father decorated, and give us roses from trees he had planted in the garden. At any moment one would not have been surprised to see the burly form of Morris himself, and the thin bearded Burne-Jones beside him, and perhaps William de Morgan walk in over the sunlit flagstones into the drawing-room. They were about the house and their memory was loved by dear May Morris. And then the aerodromes came, and the pylons and wire of electric light and the noisome dredging of the upper Thames by the Thames Conservancy, and she and Miss Lobb liked being alive less and less. Just before the war they went to Iceland together – Morris, you will remember, always went to Iceland – and soon after they returned May Morris faded out of life, and Miss Lobb soon followed her. The Manor House was left by May to Oxford University as a memorial to her father.

One final story I heard from a recent tenant of Kelmscott. This lady was sitting on a still autumn night about five years ago up on the first floor in the room which has Morris's bed in it and which leads to the tapestry room. She was alone in the house. In the silence she heard two men talking amicably in this room. She opened the door of the tapestry room to see who they were – there was no one in it. Morris? Burne-Jones? Rossetti? Philip Webb? Who knows. The place is haunting and haunted, for it has been loved as only an old house can be loved.

From the Introduction to
English Parish Churches

THE OLD CHURCHES

To atheists, inadequately developed building sites; and often, alas, to Anglicans but visible symbols of disagreement with the incumbent: 'the man there is "too high", "too low", "too lazy", "too interfering"' – still they stand, the churches of England, their towers grey above billowy globes of elm trees, the red cross of St George flying over their battlements, the Duplex Envelope System employed for collections, schoolmistress at the organ, incumbent in the chancel, scattered worshippers in the nave, Tortoise stove slowly consuming its ration as the familiar seventeenth-century phrases come echoing down arcades of ancient stone.

Odi et amo. This sums up the general opinion of the Church of England among the few who are not apathetic. One bright autumn morning I visited the church of the little silver limestone town of Somerton in Somerset. Hanging midway from a rich-timbered roof, on chains from which were suspended branched and brassy-gleaming chandeliers, were oval boards painted black. In gold letters on each these words were inscribed:

TO GOD'S
GLORY
&
THE HONOR OF
THE
CHURCH OF
ENGLAND
1782

They served me as an inspiration towards compiling this book.

The Parish Churches of England are even more varied than the landscape. The tall town church, smelling of furniture polish and hot-water pipes, a shadow of the medieval marvel it once was, so

assiduously have Victorian and even later restorers renewed every-
thing old; the little weather-beaten hamlet church standing in a
farmyard down a narrow lane, bat-droppings over the pews and one
service a month; the church of a once prosperous village, a relic of
the fifteenth-century wool trade, whose soaring splendour of stone
and glass subsequent generations have had neither the energy nor
the money to destroy; the suburban church with Northamptonshire-
style steeple rising unexpectedly above slate roofs of London and
calling with mid-Victorian bells to the ghosts of merchant carriage
folk for whom it was built; the tin chapel-of-ease on the edge of the
industrial estate; the High, the Low, the Central churches, the alive
and the dead ones, the churches that are easy to pray in and those
that are not, the churches whose architecture brings you to your
knees, the churches whose decorations affront the sight – all these
come within the wide embrace of our Anglican Church, whose arms
extend beyond the seas to many fabrics more.

From the first wooden church put up in a forest clearing or stone
cell on windy moor to the newest social hall, with sanctuary and
altar partitioned off, built on the latest industrial estate, our churches
have existed chiefly for the celebration of what some call the Mass
or the Eucharist and others call Holy Communion or the Lord's
Supper.

Between the early paganism of Britain and the present paganism
there are nearly twenty thousand churches and well over a thousand
years of Christianity. About half the buildings are medieval. Many
of those have been so severely restored in the last century that they
could almost be called Victorian – new stone, new walls, new roofs,
new pews. If there is anything old about them it is what one can
discern through the detective work of the visual imagination.

It may be possible to generalize enough about the parish church
of ancient origin to give an impression of how it is the history of its
district in stone and wood and glass. Such generalization can give
only a superficial impression. Churches vary with their building
materials and with the religious, social and economic history of their
districts.

GRAVESTONES

See on some village mound, in the mind's eye, the parish church of today. It is in the old part of the place. Near the church will be the few old houses of the parish, and almost for certain there will be an inn very near the church. A lych-gate built as a memorial at the beginning of this century indicates the entrance to the churchyard. Away on the outskirts of the town or village, if it is a place of any size, will be the arid new cemetery consecrated in 1910 when there was no more room in the churchyard.

Nearer to the church and almost always on the south side are to be found the older tombs, the examples of fine craftsmanship in local stone of the Queen Anne and Georgian periods. Wool merchants and big farmers, all those not entitled to an armorial monument on the walls inside the church, generally occupy the grandest graves. Their obelisks, urns and table tombs are surrounded with Georgian ironwork. Parish clerks, smaller farmers and tradesmen lie below plainer stones. All their families are recorded in deep-cut lettering. Here is a flourish of eighteenth-century calligraphy; there is re-produced the typeface of Baskerville. It is extraordinary how long the tradition of fine lettering continued, especially when it is in a stone easily carved or engraved, whether limestone, ironstone or slate. The tradition lasted until the middle of the nineteenth century in those country places where stone was used as easily as wood. Some old craftsman was carving away while the young go-aheads in the nearest town were busy inserting machine-made letters into white Italian marble.

The elegance of the local stone carver's craft is not to be seen only in the lettering. In the eighteenth century it was the convention to carve symbols round the top of the headstone and down the sides. The earlier examples are in bold relief, cherubs with plough-boy faces and thick wings, and scythes, hour glasses and skulls and cross-bones diversify their tops. You will find in one or another country churchyard that there has been a local sculptor of unusual vigour and perhaps genius who has even carved a rural scene above some well-graven name. Towards the end of the eighteenth century the lettering becomes finer and more prominent, the decoration flatter and more conventional, usually in the Adam manner, as though a son had taken on his father's business and depended on architectural pattern-books. But the tops of all headstones varied in shape. At this time too it became the custom in some districts to paint the stones and to add a little gold leaf to the lettering. Paint and stone by now have acquired a varied pattern produced by weather and fungus, so that the stones are probably more beautiful than they were when they were new, splodged as they are with gold and silver and slightly overgrown with moss. On a sharp frosty day when the sun is in the south and throwing up the carving, or in the west and bringing out all the colour of the lichens, a country churchyard may bring back the lost ages of craftsmanship more effectively than the church which stands behind it. Those unknown carvers are of the same race as produced the vigorous inn signs which were such a feature of England before the brewers ruined them with artiness and standardization. They had their local styles. In Kent the chief effect of variety was created by different-sized stones with elaborately scalloped heads to them, and by shroud-like mummies of stone on top of the grave itself; in the Cotswolds by carving in strong relief; in slate districts by engraved lettering. In counties like Surrey and Sussex, where stone was rare, there were many wooden graveyard monuments, two posts with a board between them running down the length of the grave and painted in the way an old wagon is painted. But most of these wooden monuments have perished or decayed out of recognition ...

THE OUTSIDE OF THE CHURCH

The church whose southern side we are approaching is probably little like the building which stood there even two centuries before, although it has not been rebuilt. The outside walls were p obably plastered, unless the church is in a district where workable stone has long been used and it is faced with cut stone known as ashlar. Churches which are ashlar-faced all over are rare, but many have an ashlar-faced western tower, or aisle to the north-east or south-east, or a porch or transept built of cut stone in the fifteenth century by a rich family. Some have a guild chapel or private chantry where

Mass was said for the souls of deceased members of the guild or family. This is usually ashlar-faced and has a carved parapet as well, and is in marked contrast with the humble masonry of the rest of the church.

Rubble or uneven flints were not considered beautiful to look at until the nineteenth century. People were ashamed of them and wished to see their churches smooth on the outside and inside walls, and weather-proof. At Barnack and Earl's Barton the Saxons have even gone so far as to imitate in stone the decorative effects of wooden construction. Plaster made of a mixture of hair or straw and sand and lime was from Saxon times applied as a covering to the walls. Only the cut stone round the windows and doors was left, and even this was lime-washed. The plaster was thin and uneven. It was beautifully coloured a pale yellow or pink or white according to the tradition of the district. And if it has now been stripped off the church, it may still be seen on old cottages of the village if any survive. The earlier the walls of a church are, the less likely they are to be ashlar-faced, for there was no widespread use of cut stone in villages until the late fourteenth century when transport was better, and attention which had formerly been expended on abbeys was paid to building and enlarging parish churches.

And this is the place to say that most of the old parish churches in England are buildings rather than architecture. They are gradual growths, as their outside walls will show; in their construction they partake of the character of cottages and barns and the early manor house, and not of the great abbey churches built for monks or secular canons. Their humble builders were inspired to copy what was to be seen in the nearest great church. The styles of Gothic came from these large buildings, but the village execution of them was later and could rarely rise to more than window tracery and roof timbering. Even these effects have a local flavour, they are a village voluntary compared with the music played on a great instrument by the cathedral organist ...

BELLS

Let us enter the church by the tower door and climb to the ringing chamber where the ropes hang through holes in the roof. Nowhere outside England except for a very few towers in the rest of the British Isles, America and the Dominions, are bells rung so well. The carillons of the Netherlands and of Bourneville are not bell ringing as understood in England. Carillon ringing is done either by means of a cylinder worked on the barrel-organ and musical-box principle, or by keyed notes played by a musician. Carillon bells are sounded by pulling the clapper to the rim of the bell. This is called chiming, and it is not ringing.

Bell ringing in England is known among ringers as 'the exercise', rather as the rearing and training of pigeons is known among the pigeon fraternity as 'the fancy'. It is a classless folk art which has survived in the church despite all arguments about doctrine and the diminution of congregations. In many a church when the parson opens with the words 'Dearly beloved brethren, the Scripture moveth us in sundry places . . .' one may hear the tramp of the ringers descending the newel stair into the refreshing silence of the graveyard. Though in some churches they may come in later by the main door and sit in the pew marked 'Ringers Only', in others they will not be seen again, the sweet melancholy notes of 'the exercise' floating out over the Sunday chimney-pots having been their contribution to the glory of God.

A belfry where ringers are keen has the used and admired look of a social club. There, above the little bit of looking-glass in which the ringers slick their hair and straighten their ties before stepping down into the outside world, you will find blackboards with gilded lettering proclaiming past peals rung for hours at a stretch. In another place will be the rules of the tower written in a clerkly hand . . . Many country towers have six bells. Not all these bells are medieval. Most were cast in the seventeenth, eighteenth or nineteenth centuries when change-ringing was becoming a country exercise. And the older bells will have been re-cast during that time, to bring them into tune with the new ones. They are likely to have been again re-cast in modern times, and the ancient inscription preserved and welded on to the re-cast bell. Most counties have elaborately produced monographs about their church bells. The older bells have beautiful lettering sometimes, as at Somerby, and South Somercotes in Lincolnshire, where they are inscribed with initial letters decorated with figures so that they look like illuminated initials from old manuscripts interpreted in relief on metal. The English love for Our Lady survived in inscriptions on church bells long after the Reformation, as did the use of Latin. Many eighteenth and even early nineteenth-century bells have Latin inscriptions. A rich collection of varied dates may be seen by struggling about on the wooden cage in which the bells hang among the bat-droppings in the tower.

Many local customs survive in the use of bells. In some places a curfew is rung every evening; in others a bell is rung at five in the morning during Lent. Fanciful legends have grown up about why they are rung, but their origin can generally be traced to the divine offices. The passing bell is rung differently from district to district. Sometimes the years of the deceased are tolled, sometimes the ringing is three strokes in succession followed by a pause. There are instances of the survival of prayers for the departed where the bell is tolled as soon as the news of the death of a parishioner reaches the incumbent.

Who has heard a muffled peal and remained unmoved? Leather bags are tied to one side of the clapper and the bells ring alternately loud and soft, the soft being an echo, as though in the next world, of the music we hear on earth.

I make no apology for writing so much about church bells. They ring through our literature, as they do over our meadows and roofs and few remaining elms. Some may hate them for their melancholy, but they dislike them chiefly, I think, because they are reminders of Eternity. In an age of faith they were messengers of consolation ...

THE INTERIOR IN 1860

In those richer days when a British passport was respected throughout the world, when 'carriage folk' existed and there was a smell of straw and stable in town streets and bobbing tenants at lodge gates in the country, when it was unusual to boast of disbelief in God and when 'Chapel' was connected with 'trade' and 'Church' with 'gentry', when there were many people in villages who had never seen a train nor left their parish, when old farm-workers still wore smocks, when town slums were newer and even more horrible, when people had orchids in their conservatories and geraniums and lobelias in the trim beds beside their gravel walks, when stained glass was brownish-green and when things that shone were considered beautiful, whether they were pink granite, brass, pitchpine, mahogany or encaustic tiles, when the rector was second only to the squire, when doctors were 'apothecaries' and lawyers 'attorneys', when Parliament was a club, when shops competed for custom, when the servants went to church in the evening, when there were family prayers and basement kitchens – in those days God seemed to have created the universe and to have sent His Son to redeem the world, and there was a church parade to worship Him on those shining Sunday mornings we read of in Charlotte M. Yonge's novels and feel in Trollope and see in the drawings in *Punch*. Then it was that the money pouring in from our empire was spent in restoring old churches and in building bold and handsome new ones in crowded areas and exclusive suburbs, in seaside towns and dockland settlements. They were built by the rich and given to the poor: 'All Seats in this Church are Free'...

THE CHURCH IN THE FIFTEENTH CENTURY

There will be no end to books on the Reformation. It is not my intention to add to them. Rather I would go back to the middle of the fifteenth century, when the church we have been describing was bright with its new additions of tower, porch, aisles and clerestory windows, and to a medieval England not quite so roseate as that of Cardinal Gasquet, nor yet so crime-ridden as that of Dr Coulton.

The village looks different. The church is by far the most prominent building unless there is a manor-house, and even this is probably a smaller building than the church and more like what we now think of as an old farm. The church is so prominent because the equivalents of cottages in the village are at the grandest 'cruck

houses' (that is to say tent-like buildings with roofs coming down
to the ground), and most are mere hovels. They are grouped round
the church and manor-house and look rather like a camp. There is
far more forest everywhere, and in all but the Celtic fringes of the
island agriculture is strip cultivation, that is to say the tilled land is
laid out in long strips with no hedges between and is common to the
whole community, as are the grazing rights in various hedged and
well-watered fields. There are more sheep than any other animals in
these enclosures. The approaches to the village are grassy tracks
very muddy in winter. Each village is almost a country to itself.
Near the entrance to the churchyard is the church house where the
church-wardens store beer or 'church ales' for feasts. This is the
origin of so many old inns being beside the churchyard in England.

The graveyard has no tombstones in it. The dead are buried there
and are remembered not in stone but in the prayers of the priest at
the altar at Mass. Everyone goes to Mass, people from outlying
farms stabling their horses outside the churchyard. The church
itself looks much the same. The stone tower gleams with new cut
ashlar; the walls of the church when they are not ashlar are
plastered.

Not only does everyone go to church on Sunday and in his best
clothes; the church is used on weekdays too, for it is impossible to
say daily prayers in the little hovels in which most of the villagers
live. School is taught in the porch, business is carried out by the
cross in the market where the booths are (for there are no shops in
the village, only open stalls as in market squares today). In the nave
of the church on a weekday there are probably people gossiping in
some places, while in others there are people praying. There was no
privacy in the Middle Ages, when even princes dined in public and
their subjects watched them eat. The nave of the church belonged
to the people, and they used it as today we use a village hall or
social club. Our new suburban churches which are used as dance
halls during the week with the sanctuary partitioned off until
Sunday, have something in common with the medieval church. But
there is this difference: in the Middle Ages all sport and pleasure,
all plays and dancing were 'under God'. God was near, hanging on
his Cross above the chancel arch, and mystically present in the

sacrament in the pyx hanging over the altar beyond. His crucifixion was carved on the preaching cross in the churchyard. People were aware of God. They were not priest-ridden in the sense that they bowed meekly to whatever the priest said. They had decided opinions and argued about religion and the clergy, and no doubt some went to church reluctantly. But no one thought of not going to church. They believed men had souls and that their souls must be exercised in worship and customed by sacraments ...

On a hot summer Sunday morning in the country, when I have been reading Chaucer to the sound of bells pouring through the trees, I have been able dimly to imagine this late medieval religion. Life is short for everybody. It is matter of fact. The pictures on the church walls are not thought of as 'art', but are there to tell a story. Small parish churches were not consciously made beautiful. They were built and decorated for effect, to be better than the church in the next village, to be the best building in the village itself, for it is the House of God, and God become Man – that was the great discovery – offered here upon the altar. All sorts of miraculous stories were invented about Him, and even more about His mother. Because He was Man born of woman, he becomes within the grasp of everyone. Few of the extravagances of German and Spanish late medieval art are found in English representations of the scourging, the crucifixion and the deposition. Jesus is thought of as the baby of poor people who received the tributes of a king. His mother is the most beautiful woman in the world – and how many lovely, loving faces of Our Lady we may see in the old glass, wall-paintings and statues which survive in England. And she bore a Spotless Son who was God and Judge of all. No wonder she was loved by the pious English.

The miracles of Our Lord were not so interesting to these peoples as the miracles they ascribed to His saints. Here extravagancy knew no bounds. St Petroc sailed in a silver bowl from Cornwall to an isle in the Indian Ocean. St Winifred was beheaded by an angry lover, but her head was reunited to her body and she became an abbess. There were saints like St Quintin who cured dropsy, saints for toothache, and for colds and fever, and for finding things. There were patron saints for every craft and trade. There were miraculous images which winked, or flew to bedsides; there were statues of saints that had never been, like the Maid Uncumber in old St Paul's Cathedral.

Though for the everyday things of life there were friendly saints who helped, life itself must have been terrifying, a continual rush to escape hell. Our Lord and His Mother were the loving and human part of it; hell was the terrifying part. The Devil was seen. His fellow devils yawned as gargoyles with bats' wings on the north walls of the church, black against the evening sky. The white teeth of devils and their red eyes gleamed out of the darkness. Evil spirits lurked behind stones on lonely moors and ranged the deep woods. Good and evil fought together in the roar of the storm. All thought, all sight, every breath of the body, was under God. The leaping sciapod, the man-eating mantichora, the unicorn, might easily be met in the forest by men with imaginations, which as easily would expect to see Our Lady flying through the air, or the local saint, for centuries enshrined in his altar, walking down the street. The witch cast her evil spells, blood and death lay around every-where, the entrails of a man hung, drawn and quartered, shone black with flies in the sun, silvery lepers tinkled their bells, creating loneliness around them. The fear that men felt is expressed in the grotesque carvings over the north walls of churches, and in the corbels and bosses of roofs, and in bench-ends, screens and miserere stalls. Their humour is shown there too. Chiefly in the figure of Our Lady do we see the tenderness and sweetness of this late religion.

So when we walk down a green lane like an ancient cart track towards the ringing church-bells, we can see the power of God in the blossom and trees, remember legends of the saints about birds and stones, and recall miracles that happened in the parish at this or that spot. And on a feast day we can see the churchyard set out with tables for the church ale when Mass is over, and as we enter the nave we can see it thronged below the painted roof and walls with people in the village, young and old, and the rest of the parish crowd-ing in with us. Human nature may not have been better. Life was as full, no doubt, of wrong and terror as it is today . . .

COMMISSIONERS' CHURCHES

By the Million Act of 1818 Parliament voted one million pounds towards the building of churches in new districts. The sentiments of the promoters of the Bill cannot have been so unlike those of Elliott*. Less charitable hearts, no doubt, terrified by the atheism consequent on the French Revolution and apprehensive of losses to landed proprietors, regarded the Million Act as a thank-offering to God for defending them from French free-thinking and continental economics. Others saw in these churches bulwarks against the rising tide of Dissent. Nearly three hundred new churches were built in industrial areas between 1819 and 1830. The Lords Commissioner of the Treasury who administered the fund required them to be built in the most economical mode, 'with a view to accommodating the greatest number of persons at the smallest expense within the compass of an ordinary voice, one half of the number to be free seats for the poor'. A limit of £20,000 was fixed for 2,000 persons. Many of these 'Commissioners' or 'Waterloo' churches, as they are now called, were built for £10,000. The most famous church of this date is St Pancras in London, which cost over £70,000. But the money was found by private subscription and a levy on the rates. For other and cheaper churches in what were then poorer districts the Commissioners contributed towards the cost.

The Commissioners themselves approved all designs. When one reads some of the conditions they laid down, it is surprising to think that almost every famous architect in the country designed churches for them – Soane, Nash, Barry, Smirke, the Inwoods, the Hardwicks, Rickman (a Quaker and the inventor of those useful terms for Gothic architecture, 'Early English', 'Decorated' and 'Perpendicular'), Cockerell and Basevi and Dobson, to name a few.

The site must be central, dry and sufficiently distant from factories and noisy thoroughfares; a paved area is to be made round the church. If vaulted underneath, the crypt is to be made available for the reception of coals or the parish fire engine. Every care must be taken to render chimneys safe from fire; they might be concealed in pinnacles. The

*Ebenezer Elliott, the Corn Law Rhymer (1781–1849).

windows ought not to resemble modern sashes; but whether Grecian or Gothic, should be in small panes and not costly. The most favourable position for the minister is near an end wall or in a semicircular recess under a half dome. The pulpit should not intercept a view of the altar, but all seats should be placed so as to face the preacher. We should recommend pillars of cast iron for supporting the gallery of a chapel, but in large churches they might want grandeur. Ornament should be neat and simple, yet variable in character.

In short, what was wanted was a cheap auditorium, and, whether Grecian or Gothic, the solution seems always to have been the same. The architects provided a large rectangle with an altar at the end in a very shallow chancel, a high pulpit on one side of the altar and a reading desk on the other, galleries round the north, west and south walls, an organ in the west gallery, and lighting from two rows of windows on the north and south walls, the lower row to light the aisles and nave, the upper to light the galleries. The font was usually under the west gallery. The only scope for invention which the architect had was in the design of portico and steeple, tower or spire.

Most large towns have at least one example of Commissioners' Churches, particularly in the north of England, where they were usually Gothic. None to my knowledge except Christ Church, Acton Square, Salford (1831) survived exactly as it was when its architect designed it. This is not because they were badly built. But they were extremely unpopular with the Victorians, who regarded them as cheap and full of shams and unworthy of the new-found dignity of the Anglican liturgy. The usual thing to do was to turn Grecian buildings into 'Byzantine' or 'Lombardic' fanes, by filling the windows with stained glass, piercing the gallery fronts with fretwork, introducing iron screens at the east end, adding a deeper chancel and putting mosaics in it, and of course cutting down the box-pews, thus ruining the planned proportions of the building and the relation of woodwork to columns supporting the galleries. The architect Sir Arthur Blomfield was a specialist in spoiling Commissioners' Churches in this way. Gothic or Classic churches were 'corrected'. In later days side chapels were tucked away in aisles originally designed for pews. Organs were invariably moved from the west galleries made for them, and were fitted awkwardly along-side the east end.

One can visualize a Commissioners' Church as it was first built, by piecing together the various undisturbed parts of these churches in different towns. The Gothic was a matter of decoration, except in St Luke's new church, Chelsea, London, and not of construction. A Commissioners' Church will be found in that part of a town where streets have names like Nelson Crescent, Adelaide Place, Regent Square, Brunswick Terrace and Hanover Villas. The streets round it will have the spaciousness of Georgian speculative building, low-terraced houses in brick or stucco, with fanlights over the doors, and, until the pernicious campaign against Georgian railings during the Nazi war, there were pleasant cast-iron verandahs on the first floor and simple railings round the planted square. Out of a wide paved space, railed in with Greek or Gothic cast iron according to the style of the building, will rise the Commissioners' Church, a brick structure with Bath stone dressings, two rows of windows and a noble entrance portico at the west end. Such churches are generally locked today, for the neighbourhood has often 'gone down'; the genteel late Georgian families who lived there moved into arboured suburbs at the beginning of this century, and their houses have been sub-let in furnished rooms.

But Commissioners' Churches, which provided worship for nearly five million people, had a dignity and coherence which we can appreciate today now that the merits of Georgian architecture are recognized. They were the last auditory buildings of the Establishment to be erected for about a century. Through the rest of the nineteenth century, most new churches might be con-sidered inauditory buildings, places where the ceremonial of the service could best be appreciated, where sight came first and sound second ...

A. W. N. PUGIN

In 1837 the Institute of British Architects was incorporated by Royal Charter. Architects were by now rather more like doctors and lawyers than artists. The most influential was Augustus Welby

Northmore Pugin (1812–52), who was said by his doctor to have crammed into his forty years of existence the work of a hundred years . . . In 1841 Pugin published his *Contrasts* and his *True Principles of Christian Architecture*. Herein he caricatured in skilful drawings the false Gothick of the Strawberry Hill type, and lampooned everything that was classical. To contrast with these he made beautiful shaded drawings of medieval buildings, particularly those of the late fourteenth century. He did not confine his carica-tures to architecture, and peopled the foregrounds with figures. In front of pagan or classical buildings he drew indolent policemen, vulgar tradesmen and miserable beggars; before the medieval buildings he drew vested priests and pious pilgrims. He idealized the Middle Ages. His drawings were sincere but unfair. The prose accompaniment to them is glowing and witty.

Pugin's own churches, which were almost all Roman Catholic, are attempts to realize his dreams. But for all the sincerity of their architect, the brass coronals, the jewelled glass by Hardman of Birmingham, the correctly moulded arches and the carefully carved woodwork have a spindly effect. St Chad's Roman Catholic Cathedral at Birmingham, St Augustine's Church, Ramsgate, and St Giles's, Cheadle, are exceptions. It is not in his buildings but in his writing that Pugin had so great an influence on the men of his time.

Pugin is sometimes supposed to have joined the Church of Rome for aesthetic reasons only. It is true that he saw in it the survival of the Middle Ages to which he desired the world to return. But the Roman Catholics of his time were not whole-heartedly in favour of the Gothic style he advocated, and to his annoyance continued to build in the classic style of the Continent or else in the plaster-thin Gothick he despised. The Church of England, newly awakened to its Catholicism, took more kindly to his doctrines, so that although he came in for some mild criticism from *The Ecclesiologist* (the organ first of the Cambridge Camden Society, and from 1845 of Catholic-minded Anglicans in general), Pugin contemplated writing an essay called: 'An Apology for the separated Church of England since the reign of the Eighth Henry. Written with every feeling of Christian charity for her Children, and honour of the glorious men she continued to produce in evil times. By A. Welby Pugin, many years a Catholic-minded son of the Anglican Church, and still an affectionate and loving brother of the true sons of England's Church.'

I do not think it was solely for aesthetic reasons, or even for doctrinal reasons, that Pugin joined the Church of Rome. He possessed what we now call a 'social conscience'. He deplored the slums he saw building round him. He abhorred the soullessness of machinery, and revered hand craftsmanship. His drawings of industrial towns contrasted with a dream-like Middle Ages, his satire on the wealthy ostentation of a merchant's house – 'On one side of the house machicolated parapets, embrasures, bastions, and all the show of strong defence, and round the corner of the building a conservatory leading to the principal rooms, through which a whole company of horsemen might penetrate at one smash into the heart of the mansion! – for who would hammer against nailed portals when he could kick his way through the greenhouse?' – are summed up in the two principles of Gothic or Christian architecture which he delivered to the world. These are they. 'First, that there should be no features about a building which are not necessary for convenience, construction, or propriety; second, that all ornament should consist of enrichment of the essential construction of the building.' Pugin's principle, and his conviction that the only style that was Christian was Gothic, are fathered by popular opinion on Ruskin. But Ruskin was not fond of Pugin. He disliked his Popery, and he thought little of his buildings. If one must find a successor to Pugin, it is the eventual atheist William Morris. Both men liked simplicity and good craftsmanship. Both had a 'social conscience'. Pugin dreamed of a Christian world, Morris of a Socialist world, but both their worlds were dreams...

MODERN TIMES

See in your mind's eye a church built in the neo-Perpendicular style by G. G. Scott junior, Bodley, W. H. Bidlake of Birmingham, Edgar Wood, Sir Ninian Comper, W. D. Caroë, Sir Charles Nicholson, Temple Moore, J. D. Sedding, Edmund Sedding,

Charles Spooner, E. P. Warren, Walter Tapper, Niven and Wiggles-worth, Austin and Paley, to name a few of these later Victorian architects. If you cannot see it, I will try to re-create such a church, and you will remember it in some newish suburb of a provincial town where you stayed with an aunt, or on a holiday in the outskirts of a south-coast watering place, and you can read of it in Compton Mackenzie's *Sinister Street*. 'Ting-ting' the single bell calls to Sung Eucharist, because the tower, designed for a full peal of bells, was never completed. Rather gaunt without it, the church rises above the privet and forsythia and prunus of its little garden, for there is no churchyard to these churches; we have reached the era of municipal cemeteries, and it is in their marble acres that the dead of this new parish are to be found. Inside the church, the tall nave is filled with chairs, and the narrow aisles are not used on a Sunday, as they give a view only of side altars where the weekday Celebrations and the very early Sunday Masses are said. The floor is of oak blocks, the walls are cream and clean, the woodwork of the thick Devonshire-styled chancel screen, carved by Harry Hems of Exeter, is unstained. In more recent times a coloured statue of Our Lady under a gilded canopy is seen against one of the eastern-most pillars of the nave. Through the screen we glimpse a huge reredos painted green and red and gold, with folding doors. The high altar has a purple frontal, because just now it is Lent. The floor of the sanctuary is paved with black-and-white marble. Riddel posts with gilt angels on them – the famous 'English altar' introduced by Sir Ninian Comper in the nineties – hold curtains round the north, south and east of the side altars. The windows are filled with greenish glass in which are patches of dark blue, red and gold. These are the work of Kempe, and they allow more light into the church than earlier Victorian windows. The chief beauty of the church is its proportion. These architects favoured two kinds of proportion when they were building in the Gothic style – almost all of them designed Byzantine and classic churches as well – and they were either height and narrowness, or breadth and length. Their churches either soar or spread.

The Sung Eucharist is probably from the Prayer Book and with a crowd of acolytes at the altar. Blue incense rises to the golden reredos and the green Kempe window. The English Hymnal is used, and plain-song or, more probably, Eyre in E♭ or Tours in C. Candlelights twinkle in the mist. The purple Lenten chasuble of the priest is worn over amice, alb, stole and maniple, and there is discussion of these things after the service and before among servers and the initiated. We are in a world which feels itself in touch with the Middle Ages and with today. This is English Catholicism. There is much talk of Percy Dearmer, correct furnishings and vestments, the Prayer Book and how far one is justified in departing from it. After church the acolytes in their Sunday suits hang round the porch, and the young curates too, and there is a good deal of backslapping and chaff. For months the Mothers' Union and the women's guilds of the church have been working on banners and a frontal to be ready for Easter. From these suburban parishes much of the Church life of modern England has sprung. They have trained their people in faith and the liturgy, they have produced many of the overseas missionaries and parish priests of today.

We are in modern times, out of the older and rich suburbs with their garden city atmosphere of guild craftsmen and Sarum Use, and into the big building estates. These large areas of semi-detached houses, built by private speculators or councils, have been eating up our agricultural land since 1920. They have been brought about by the change in transport from steam to motor-bus and electric train. People are moving out of the crowded early-Victorian industrial lanes and terraces, into little houses of their own, each with its little patch of garden at the back and front, each isolated from its neighbour by social convention, in districts where miles of pavement enlivened by the squeak of perambulators lead to a far-off bus route and parade of chain stores, and a distant Vita-glass school, used as a Community Centre in the evenings. To these places, often lonely for all the people in them, comes the new mission Church.

Just as there is today no definite modern style in England, except in what is impermanent – exhibition buildings, prefabs, holiday camps and the like – so there is no definite modern church style. In the period between the two wars church architects were too often concerned with style, and they built places of worship which vied with the local Odeon or with by-pass modern factories in trying to be 'contemporary'. They now look dated, and will, I fear, never look beautiful. But the purpose of the church remains the same as it always was, to be a place where the Faith is taught and the Sacraments are administered.

Middlesex

I was walking down a High Road in the gallant County of Middlesex on a hot Saturday morning. Black glass fascias of chain stores, each at a different height from its neighbour, looked like rows of shiny goloshes on the feet of buildings. Corner shops and supermarkets seemed to be covered in coloured plastic, like the goods they sold. All too soon the wrappings would be torn off and left to blow about municipal rose beds and recreation grounds. Somewhere, if I dared to raise my eyes above the crowded pavement, there must have been sky, but between it and me were concrete lamp standards, the tops of buses and enormous lorries carrying mattresses, and bulk liquids, or dragging trailers full of chassis of motor-cars. On the other side of the road, where once there had been a gap between two red-brick parades of Edwardian shops, there used to be a cottage with a glimpse of orchard behind. This is now filled by a chain store about a quarter of an acre in extent. Wares were called out in so many varieties of lettering and colour – shops where you could buy do-it-yourself kits, television shops, refrigerator shops, bedding and furniture stores – that the riot of display called for a sixth sense to distinguish which was which. And out, beyond the centre of the place, if this long straggle could be said to have a centre, there used to be three-storey brick Italianate villas with large front gardens. These gardens are now full of second-hand motor-cars for sale and piles of tyres. The stench and noise were terrific; diesel from lorries and buses, the subtly differing horrors of various brands of petrol in private cars and, over all, the continuous roar of aeroplanes circling into London Airport. Far louder than this was the detonation of ton-up boys freed by the five-day week, while transistor sets on the pavement competed with other programmes from the television shops.

This is Middlesex. This was the county which inspired Keats when he stood tiptoe on a hilltop and heard

> A little noiseless noise among the leaves,
> Born of the very sigh that silence heaves.

This is the new world which over-population, abetted by big business and 'developers', has created. This is what every county in southern England and a good many in the north and midlands will soon become. Probably there is no turning back and for that reason every acre where there is still quiet and the smell of grass and the sound of brooks becomes more precious and essential for our recreation.

Like many others, I can recall that Middlesex High Road before the onslaught which started in the thirties and has gained pace in the fifties and sixties. There were still chemists' shops, with big coloured bottles behind their *art nouveau* glazing bars, and, inside, the rows of coloured jars on mahogany shelves; there were linen drapers where the change ran in a wooden ball from the counter to the cash desk on a rail among handkerchiefs and lace; dairies, lined with blue and white tiles, were adorned with a polished churn and a china cow; the sweet smell of baking came from bread shops; butchers' shops were open to the straw and dust of the highroad, and along that highroad was the occasional chug of a motor-car, the clop of horse hooves and the hiss and grind of the electric tramcar beneath its overhead wires.

I don't say the High Road was more hygienic than it is now, but I do say it was pleasanter and one could sleep in a house looking over it without the united aid of sleeping pills, ear plugs and double glazing. One knew, too, that between the main roads into London were still a few hay fields, market gardens and dairy farms which supplied London with fodder and fresh food. It was possible to walk from Edgware to Harrow past little farms and down lanes heavy with may. In West Middlesex between Uxbridge and Staines were country houses with garden walls of that rich, dark, brown-and-red Middlesex brick, little wooded parks, cedar-shaded lawns and miniature lakes. Each was the *rus in urbe* of some Georgian townee set up as squire, whose monuments with carved arms and cherubs and flowery epitaphs adorned the walls of the parish churches from Tottenham to Stanwell. There were farms with weatherboard barns, such as the mighty barn which still survives at Harmondsworth, orchards and gardens of clipped box and yew. There were village greens and inns like that which unexpectedly remains, church, inn and all, at Norwood Green near the farmland round Osterley and the banks of the Brent, so near to London that you can see above enormous elms the flashing factory towers of the Great West Road. Middlesex today still has just under 30,000 acres of crops, rough grass and pasture, and it has 7,000 cows. This is all that remains of the richest agricultural land near London.

It is easy to see in terms of transport how the invasion of Middlesex occurred. First the nearer villages to London succumbed, those within gig distance from the City. Then the steam trains added their grey-brick station roads to larger villages like Edmonton, Enfield, Ealing, Twickenham and Hampton, and increased the importance of towns such as Brentford and Staines. They drew industry from East London to Willesden. Electric traction by tram and railway beyond enticed people out of London to the west and north-west of the little county. Buses and motor-cars have filled remaining gaps. Now only on its northern borders, by South Mimms and Forty Hill, and in the north-west, between Harefield and Ruislip, and here and there among the reservoirs and aerodromes of the Hundred of Spelthorne, can any pockets of country be found.

Most of the delicate attractions of the county, old brick walls, inns and farm buildings, survive close up to its parish churches. To the county local authorities, and those very few landowners who have withstood the blandishments of 'developers', we owe the identity of Middlesex as a county at all. Unless there is public will to preserve and maintain the wild and natural, the old and gentle, then all the Home Counties will suffer the same fate.

Cornwall

When I first came to Cornwall over fifty years ago, as a small boy, we drove the seven miles from the station in a horse-brake; there was only one motor-car in the parish and this could not attempt the steeper hills. Roads were only partially metalled and in the lesser lanes the rock showed through on the surface. Everyone in the village had oil lamps and candles. A journey to the nearest town and back was a day's expedition. There were still many country people who had never been to London and the story used to be told of one of them who thought the metropolis was all under a glass roof because he never got further than Paddington Station. Visitors to Cornwall, 'foreigners' as they are rightly called by the Cornish, were mostly fishermen, golfers and artists. My own father, in his leisure from business in London, was all three.

The attraction of Cornish scenery for artists started with the picturesque movement at the end of the eighteenth century. Thomas Rowlandson used to stay with the Onslows at Hengar in St Tudy parish and sketch the wooded valleys of north Cornwall, the tors on Bodmin Moor, the churches, farms and cliffs. He set a fashion which other English watercolour artists and engravers followed, notably Thomas Daniell. In the 1820s Turner found inspiration in the south coast of the Duchy. By the 1880s artists were coming from England into Cornwall and settling in St Ives and Newlyn and painting not only the scenery but the people.

Some, like Stanhope Forbes, made the journey via Brittany. The first whorls of the silvery mist of the Celtic Revival had risen at Tintagel with Tennyson's *Idylls of the King*. The Cornish Celtic Revivalists, poetical and artistic, took an interest in the old Cornish language which was akin to Breton and Welsh and had died out in the eighteenth century, and in the legends of the Celtic saints. The poet Hawker sang of the saints in Morwenstow, and the indefatigable Baring-Gould told and sometimes invented picturesque legends about Celtic saints, later to be corrected by the learned

Celtic hagiographer, Canon Doble. The revival of the see of Cornwall and the building of the cathedral in Truro in the eighties turned the gaze of Christians to Brittany, where the feasts of so many Cornish saints were still kept.

The romantic view of the Cornish and Cornwall has continued until the present day. The accomplished work of the Victorian artists of the Newlyn and St Ives schools is just being appreciated again, after nearly half a century's neglect. Stanhope Forbes's paintings show the Londoner's delight in the simple life, fisherfolk and the stony Celtic cottages and fields.

From the eighteenth century Opie to Peter Lanyon in the present there have, of course, been noted native artists. The Cornish themselves are not dreamy and unpractical as the 'foreigners' sometimes suppose. Like most Celts, they combine a deep sense of religion with a shrewd gift for business. These iron age people, who were Christian before the Saxons, had, until they were discovered by the tourists in the last century, a hard struggle for existence. The Saxons and the Normans tried to hold them down with forts and castles. They did not take kindly to the Reformation, nor to Cromwell, and most of them stood out for King Charles. They gained their living, since Roman times, by mining, for the minerals of Cornwall are numerous and rich, and he who buys land there likes to buy the mining rights too. They were also farmers and fishermen. Their religious faith was awakened in the eighteenth century by John Wesley and to this day the majority of the Cornish are Methodists. They had their own brand of it in the Bible Christians, a sect whose chief light was Billy Bray, the converted tin miner. Many an oil-lit chapel rang with alleluyas on a Sunday and hearts were lifted at the thought of a glorious day coming in the next life after years of ill-paid toil in the hot labyrinths of the mines. Their practical gifts came out in the invention of machinery for pumping water out of the mines and the use of steam power. They were boatbuilders, craftsmen and engineers, rather than architects. For this reason the buildings of Cornwall are mostly homely and not at all grand. Only a Cornishman would have the endurance to carve intractable granite as he has done at St Mary Magdalene, Launceston, and Probus tower.

The awakening of the Cornish to the value of the tourist industry came with the railways. The Great Western extended itself into Cornwall and was thought of first in terms of goods traffic – tin, china clay and fish. The London & South-Western, the Great Western's rival, ran a line into north Cornwall via Okehampton, largely for holiday traffic. Fathers who had come for the fishing and mothers who wanted sea air for their families at cheaper rates and in less plebeian conditions than those provided in Thanet or Brighton came to Cornwall. Monster hotels were built at the beginning of this century to provide for them, such as the King Arthur's Castle at Tintagel, the Poldhu at Mullion and the Metropole at Padstow. Many a terrace of boarding houses arose in seaports which had hitherto thought that their only industry was to be fishing. Newquay and Bude are largely 'foreigners'' creations, and Falmouth, turning the corner westward of Pendennis Castle, built a new seaside town. Simultaneously with the big hotel came the early twentieth-century cult of the old cottage in the country, and picturesque ports like Polperro, St Ives, Looe and Fowey did well. Farmers' wives specialized in Cornish teas and fishermen rowed the 'foreigners' out of the harbour to catch mackerel they would otherwise be catching themselves. Farmers on the sea coast started growing bungalows instead of wheat.

All this tourist industry brought prosperity and security to Cornwall until the appearance of the Duchy was seriously altered by electricity and the motor-car. The Electricity Board has strung the fields, villages and towns of Cornwall with more poles and wires, ill-sited and clumsily arranged, than in any other part of the British Isles. This is partly because even the remotest bungalow on a cliff wants electricity and partly because burying cables in slate or granite is expensive. The motor-car has made the greatest change of all. Roads have been widened, blocks of houses have been taken down in picturesque ports to make way for car parks; petrol stations proliferate; huge hoardings to attract the motorist line the entrances to towns. In the holiday season lorries and cars trailing caravans and boats block lanes never intended for such heavy traffic. The County Planning authorities, hard put to it to find available sites on the coast, have been obliged to introduce caravans and chalets even to the wooded inland valleys. Several stretches of the coast have been rescued by the National Trust or saved, at any rate for their life-time, by those landowners who can still afford to hold out against the blandishment of 'developers'. The old and beautiful Cornwall is now mostly to be found on foot or in a small car by those skilled in using the one-inch ordnance survey map. It is a consolation that no one yet has discovered how to build houses on the sea.

Early English

Higher than the forest trees, nobler than the barons' castles, the English monasteries of the thirteenth century soared heavenward in stone. They were the beginning of a national style. We call it Early English and it grew out of the round-arched Norman style.

The names for the architectural styles of medieval England were devised by a Quaker architect, Thomas Rickman, in 1817, and they have stuck. He called Romanesque Norman. The style which might be called Early Pointed, when people were just beginning to find out about the pointed arch, he called Transitional. This was followed by Early English, Decorated and Perpendicular. Each style lasted roughly a century. The Early English lasted from 1150 to 1250, that is to say through the reigns of Henry II, Richard I, John and Henry III, a period when the King and the barons were less powerful than the Church, and when England was still closely connected with Northern France. Churches were therefore the most prominent buildings. They rose, many steepled, out of walled cities. Lincoln must have looked superb on its hill when the three towers of its cathedral were finally completed with spires in the fourteenth century. The west front of Wells (1240) was a sculpture gallery of outdoor figures ranged in long rows in niches. The whole of this west front of Wells was painted in many colours, so that it must have seemed as startling as an oriental temple would today if it were standing over the Somerset meadows.

The Early English style usually has acutely pointed arches, slender columns, sometimes clustered together like pipes of stone, and, on the top of the columns, capitals, very often carved with leaves and forming a bell shape. The mouldings of the arches are deep and you can put your hand right into them. Salisbury, Lincoln, Wells and Worcester are cathedrals which are outstanding examples of the Early English style, though many other cathedrals exhibit it. Parish churches are sometimes in the Early English style. For instance, one of the finest is West Walton in Norfolk, and another is

Abbey Dore in Herefordshire. A third is Uffington in Berkshire. Where a parish church has Early English features, whether it be a chancel window or an arcade, you can generally be certain that the church was connected with an abbey which supplied its priests and caused it to be built. Sometimes a rich abbey would build, even bigger than the church, a barn in the district, where it collected its tithes from the farmers. The Abbey of Beaulieu, in Hampshire, built the great stone barn of Great Coxwell in Berkshire in the thirteenth century. The monasteries and convents were really the equivalent of large industries today: they drew people to them and they supplied work.

When we are told in the guide book that Bishop So and So built this or that part of a cathedral or a church, the actual work of building was done by the master mason. John Harvey, the architectural writer, has found out the names of many of these medieval masons. They moved from job to job and their styles can be recognized. Nothing is known about them personally. We shall not know what, in about 1200, gave the designer of the famed west front of Peterborough Cathedral the brilliant idea of making the central of his three great arches smaller than those which flank it. At the time the custom had been to reverse that arrangement – a large arch in the middle and smaller ones at the sides.

Medieval men were smaller in stature than we are today. They lived in squalid wooden cottages with earth floors in front of clearings in the forest. These were their villages, and they stayed in the monasteries very often when they worked for the monks on the building of the abbeys. That they should have produced such splendid and complete buildings as Salisbury and Lincoln and Wells and Worcester in the Early English style is a source of wonder. There are various reasons. Firstly it was an age of great faith and building was a pleasure and there were fewer distractions than now. And secondly the Church must have been a calmer and more regular taskmaster than the hunting barons, who had gone off on Crusades against the infidels.

The most rational explanation of the origin of Early English Gothic and therefore of the Gothic style generally, the style of the pointed arch, is the necessity to roof an oblong space with stone.

Wooden roofs were always catching alight. Chartres Cathedral was burned in 1020, Vézelay in 1120. In 1174, four years after the murder of Becket, the newly completed choir of Canterbury was burned to the ground amid the groans of the monks, who cursed God and their patron saints for allowing such a thing to happen. William of Sens was the architect called from France to rebuild the choir of Canterbury in 1175. For three years it was rebuilding and he re-roofed it in stone in the French way. He was roofing in what is called sexpartite vaulting, that is to say he was using a pointed arch instead of a round arch. This had already been attempted over the choir of Durham Cathedral.

The Normans knew about vaulting a square space. They used the old Roman method of quadripartite vaulting, that is to say two stone half cylinders of equal height crossing one another at right angles. When you have to vault an oblong space in stone obviously one pair of arches is going to be larger than the other pair, therefore the only thing to do is to pinch up the smaller pair until it is as high as the larger pair. This brings about the pointed arch. The vaulting is thus divided into six and the compartments are separated by stone ribs. At Durham you can see this crudely attempted; the point is there and the detail still takes one back to the old days of the Romanesque. In Canterbury you still have a sense of France and the Romanesque in the columns of the choir; but the vaulting above, with the thin ribs of stone, is without a hint of the Romanesque style about it. If you want to see what the roofs of Norman churches were like when they were of wood and before the stone vaulting of oblong spaces had been discovered, then Peterborough Cathedral nave has the largest painted Romanesque wooden roof in Europe. The Early English style of the pointed stone vaulting of a nave carried to perfection is to be found at Salisbury and Wells – and best of all at Lincoln. These three cathedrals are very much in the English style, and are not like the choir of Canterbury, which is distinctly French.

A way of vaulting an oblong space which was much used on the Continent in Romanesque days was to create a barrel vault, that is to say one long half cylinder of stone running down the whole length of the nave as a roof. But, of course, such a roof exerted very strong outward pressure on the walls, as did the steep-pitched wooden roofs of earlier churches and halls. However, as soon as you point the arches and distribute the thrust of the stone at certain points along the wall, instead of all along the wall, you can have much thinner walls between large buttresses which counteract the thrust of the stone vaulting. Thus the walls of the new churches like Lincoln Cathedral, Salisbury Cathedral and Wells have large buttresses along them; but between the buttresses the walls can be fairly thin. Even in Norman times, before they discovered pointed arches for stone vaulting, they had been enlarging the little windows high up into large round-headed windows. Now that they had discovered that walls could be thinner they also enlarged the windows. In fact every monastery and every parish church that could afford it wanted to rebuild in the new pointed style.

Monasteries and churches – with the single exception of Salisbury, which was all built in the thirteenth century, except for its spire, which is a century later – are the gradual growths of centuries and they are built in the form of addition upon addition. The new pointed style could rise higher than the Romanesque churches and the buildings could be broader. As it was extremely important that the services should continue uninterrupted in the choirs of the cathedrals while the building was going on, the extensions were made round them. The fact is that they were always adding to them, particularly at the east end, where they had the shrines of the saints. This system of building additions all the time accounts for the great length of English cathedrals, and the way one aisle leads into another, and transept leads to chapel, and chapel gives a glimpse of yet another chapel.

The new style, Early English, was sculpture become architecture. It was as though the Saxons had been allowed to use their chisels and had ousted the rough axed surface decoration of the Normans. And as the style went on, carving abounded: carved capitals on the tops of columns, with leaves, or things that looked like leaves, springing from them. In fact, it was, in every sense of the word, the springtime of architecture. Great delight was taken by carvers of corbels and capitals in introducing little figures, peasants, listening monks, boys, bears, pigs, nuns, gossips.

The larger windows let in more light on to the carving. The pieces of glass leaded together in these large windows were still small and the prevailing colours, where figures were introduced, were blue, olive green, deep red and brownish pink for depicting human flesh, and very black outlines. There was much grisaille, that is to say silvery-grey glass, in the tall Early English windows. No Early English cathedrals or churches today have the complete decorative scheme that they had when they were built, though the Victorians made some gallant attempts to recreate them. We can only get an idea of what they looked like from fragments of painting on walls, and from glass, where it survives.

When Sir Gilbert Scott, the Victorian cathedral restorer, was working at Salisbury with his son George Gilbert Scott Junior, they found a lot of the colour in the nave and choir behind the white-wash with which the cathedral had been adorned inside. George Gilbert Scott Junior says:

The ruling intention appears to have been to have coloured window glass and richly coloured wall-spaces. The stained glass, of which a few fragments have escaped the vandalism of the Puritans and the stupidity of the chapter, was remarkable both by absence of figurework and the unusual predominance of white glass. The walls, on the contrary, were painted a full red, relieved by bold scroll work in black, and the mouldings were decorated upon the same system.

Thus the marble work, instead of showing, as it now does, almost black upon white, was designed to be in perfect tone, as regards chiaroscuro, with the red and the black of the wall-spaces. The only parts in which white was employed as a ground were the vaultings, the ribs of which were decorated in full colour, while the inter-spaces were occupied by medallions, in which red is again the predominating tint.

The red was of that brownish earth colour sometimes seen on the walls of old country churches.

A pilgrimage to a shrine in one of these new abbey churches must have been a startling series of experiences – the journey through the wild country, the resting at an inn provided by the monastery, the way out of the ordinary world marked by a great screen of stone images across the west front of the abbey, as at Wells and Salisbury and Lincoln. Then the pilgrim walked under this screen through a comparatively low door out of the light into unimaginable painted wonder, seen in the mitigated light of silvery glass. There were twinkling altars and statues everywhere, a sense of vista beyond vista, the monks screened off in their stalls chanting as one passed by on the way to the shrine of the saint, expecting a miracle and a blessing. There was an attempt in these Early English Gothic abbeys and churches to create a semblance of Heaven on earth, with their stone, colour, music and ritual. We go to foreign lands as the people of the Middle Ages went to cathedrals. And to them they must have seemed more impressive than our first sight of New York to us.

St Pancras

St Pancras was a fourteen-year-old Christian boy, who was martyred in Rome in AD 304 by the Emperor Diocletian. In England he is better known as a railway station. That station takes its name from the parish in which it stands. It is the terminus of the Midland Railway, the most mid-Victorian of all British lines. It wasn't the fastest line but it was the most comfortable, and was the first to introduce a dining car and upholstered seats for third-class passengers. Its livery was scarlet. Scarlet were the famous Kirtley engines with their black funnels; scarlet the carriages and scarlet enlivened with stone dressings and polished granite the walls of the mighty terminus and hotel of St Pancras. So strong is the personality of this station to a Londoner that he does not remember the medieval but mercilessly restored local church, nor the chaste Greek revival St Pancras church in the Euston Road, nor even St Pancras Town Hall opposite the station, now renamed Camden Town Hall. What he sees in his mind's eye is that cluster of towers and pinnacles seen from Pentonville Hill and outlined against a foggy sunset and the great arc of Barlow's train shed gaping to devour incoming engines, and the sudden burst of the exuberant Gothic of the hotel seen from gloomy Judd Street.

The Midland Railway did not reach London until 1867 for goods and 1868 for passengers. Its headquarters and its heart were always in Derby. It used to run trains into Kings Cross by arrangement with the Great Northern Railway. Its other rival from the midlands was the long established London & North Western at Euston next door. This was always a belligerent and uncooperative company. If the Midland was to have a terminus in London, it must be a contrast with its neighbours – not old fashioned Greek and Graeco-Roman like Euston with its Doric portico and Great Hall, not mere engineering like grimy stock brick Kings Cross, but something to show that the midlands and the Midland had plenty of brass and were not old-fashioned. Bringing the line to London

avoiding its competitors was difficult enough, and when the out-
skirts of the metropolis were reached it was harder still. After
burrowing through the Middlesex hills at Hampstead it had to cross
a canal. Should it tunnel under this, as the Great Northern and the
London & North Western had done, or should it cross it by a
bridge? It decided to bridge the canal. In order to do this the very
large and very crowded burial ground of old St Pancras would have
to be levelled. When the work started, skulls and bones were seen
lying about; a passer-by saw an open coffin staved in through which
peeped a bright tress of hair. Great scandal was caused and the
company was forced to arrange for reverent reburial. The architect
in charge of the reburial was A. W. Blomfield, and he sent one of
his assistants to watch the carrying away of the dead to see that it
was reverently done. That assistant was Thomas Hardy, and his
poems 'The Levelled Churchyard' and 'In the Cemetery' recall
the fact. Once when he and Blomfield met on the site they found a
coffin which contained two skulls.

> O Passenger, pray list and catch
> Our sighs and piteous groans,
> Half stifled in this jumbled patch
> Of wrenched memorial stones!
>
> We late-lamented, resting here,
> Are mixed to human jam,
> And each to each exclaims in fear,
> 'I know not which I am!'

Hardy never forgot the event.

The Midland also had to clear a horrible slum district at Agar
Town and part of the equally depressed Somers Town. The in-
habitants were not properly rehoused. Yet on came the Midland,
full of brass and assurance. It tunnelled one line down to join the
Metropolitan (steam) Underground Railway, which is now part of
the Inner Circle, and, from Farringdon Street, trains could enter the
City or cross the river at Blackfriars. Most of its lines at St Pancras
stopped short at the Euston Road, but as it had had to cross the
canal by a bridge, the station ended high in air above the Euston
Road. This gave its engineer William Henry Barlow (1812–1902) a

chance to build what remained for nearly a century, the largest station roof in the world without internal supports. It also inspired him to build what is still the most practical terminus in London. The great cast-iron arched ribs which support the roof were made by the Butterley Iron Company, whose name appears in white on a blue background on each rib above the platforms, reminding us of the Derbyshire origin of the line. The ribs are tied together by floor girders over which the trains run. To increase wind resistance the great curved arch of the station is slightly broken at its apex, so that it is almost a Gothic arch. This whole structure rests on a forest of iron columns under the station. The exterior fence of this forest is the brick wall of the station and hotel. The Midland made good use of the ground-floor level under its terminus. Much of the trade of the line was beer from Burton-on-Trent, and the distance between the iron columns was measured by the length of beer barrels, which were carried down here from the station above by hydraulic lifts, and taken by drays out into London. This gloomy area, when it ceased to be used for beer, became a lair of wild cats. It is now partly a National Car Park and partly the haunt of motor repairing firms. A few shops survive with Gothic windows to them along Euston Road and Pancras Road.

When Barlow designed the train shed, he made provision for an hotel to be built in front of it, above the Euston Road. The station and hotel are approached by ramps, one steep and the other a gentle double curve, so that to this day St Pancras is the most practically designed station for ambulances and certainly the most considerate and humane to mobile passengers. The station was completed in 1868 and Barlow constructed glass screens at either end of his train shed. That on the Euston Road side was designed to keep smoke and noise from the projected hotel. The hotel was started in the year the station was completed, and it was opened to the public in 1873. At the time it was easily the most magnificent of all London hotels. It was one of the first to have lifts, called 'ascending rooms' and worked by hydraulic power. It was also one of the first to have electric bells. It could be a fine hotel again. The architect was the most eminent man of his time, Sir Gilbert Scott (1811–1878). Scott was of course the envy of his profession. This is one of the reasons

why the *avant garde* architectural critics of the seventies con-
demned the building as a 'monster'. It may also be a reason for the
totally false rumour which I once believed myself, that St Pancras
was the Gothic design Scott made for the Foreign Office in 1856,
and which Palmerston rejected. Having studied both designs and
the plans for them, there is no resemblance except in style. It must
be remembered that in the 1860s Gothic was the equivalent of what
used to be called 'contemporary' in the 1950s. Any promising
architect and go-ahead company would insist on Gothic if they
wanted to be thought up to date.

For the last ninety years almost, Sir Gilbert Scott has had a bad
press. He is condemned as facile, smart, aggressive, complacent and
commercial. When at the top of his form Scott was as good as the
best of his Gothic contemporaries. He was so firm a believer in the
Gothic style as the only true 'Christian' style – Scott was a moder-
ate High Churchman – that he was determined to adapt it for
domestic and commercial purposes. St Pancras station hotel was
his greatest chance in London and well he rose to the occasion.

I used to think that Scott was a rather dull architect, but the
more I have looked at his work the more I have seen his merits. He
had a thorough knowledge of construction, particularly in stone and
brick. For St Pancras the bricks were specially made by Edward
Gripper in Nottingham. The decorative iron work for lamp
standards and staircases and grilles was by Skidmore of Coventry,
who designed the iron screens in some English cathedrals for Scott.
The roofs of the hotel are of graded Leicestershire slates; the stone
comes mostly from Ketton. Scott's buildings are so well-built they
are difficult to pull down. He had a grand sense of plan and site. The
hotel building consists of refreshment and dining-rooms at station
level on the ground floor, and wine cellars in the basement. The
Grand Staircase, which alone survives of the hotel's chief interior
features, ascends the whole height of the building, by an un-
believably rich cast iron series of treads with stone vaulting and
painted walls. The chief suites of rooms are on the first floor and the
higher the building, the less important the rooms, until the quarters
for the servants are reached in the gabled attics – men on one side,
women on the other – and separate staircases. Yet even these are

large and wide and compare favourably with more modern accommodation. The building has been chopped up and partitioned inside for offices. It is odd that it is not used again as an hotel especially now that hotels are so badly needed in London.

Scott had full confidence in being able to exploit the site. The chief rooms are on the front and look across to the once level plains of Bloomsbury and up and down the Euston Road. Even on the first floor they are sufficiently high to be out of the noise of traffic. For the external effect of his hotel Scott used the same technique as Barry had done for the Houses of Parliament, that is to say he increased the sense of height on the comparatively low setting by having a steep roof and many towers and spirelets. Such things always look well in our grey climate. He meant to put Euston and Kings Cross to shame. For the rear of his hotel, where it faced the station, he put service rooms and backstairs and made the brick exterior plain, since it was mostly submerged in the train shed. Above the train shed it rises into gables.

There was at one time a serious threat to St Pancras, both as a station and an hotel. Puritans of the thirties were prepared to allow merit to Barlow's train shed, because it was simple and functional. Scott's hotel, however, filled them with horror, because its exterior was ornate and its style they considered sham medieval. If you look again at the hotel you will see it is not sham. It uses brick of the best quality and cast iron, and its proportions bear no resemblance to a medieval domestic building – no medieval building, not even an Hôtel de Ville, of that size was ever built. There still survive along the Euston Road some ingenious façades Scott has constructed for shop fronts in the low brick arches under the station. Today we can appreciate Sir Gilbert's masterpiece. For grandeur of scale it compares with that best work of Sir Gilbert's grandson Sir Giles, Liverpool Cathedral.

The architectural department of British Railways has not tried to have St Pancras station cleaned, and has allowed mean hoardings for advertisements to deface the interior of the station, and to be placed without any regard for the vertical lines created by Scott and Barlow. Mingy little notices and cumbersome new electric lamps are stuck about without regard to proportion or the façades. The now old-fashioned with-itry of the fifties, which has given us the slabs and cubes of high finance, and ruined most of London, has made St Pancras all the more important to us for the relief it brings. It shows that trouble was taken and money spent in its building.

There is one more most important thing to be said in favour of St Pancras station. This was said to me at a party I attended for the publication of Jack Simmons's readable, learned and inspiring book *St Pancras Station*. I was introduced to three former Station Masters of St Pancras, a succession going back to the 1914 war. They all said how magnificent the station was, how fond they were of it, and the last one added, 'moreover *it works*'.

Postscript *from* Highworth

When I am abroad and want to recall a typically English town, I think of Highworth. Countless unknown lanes lead up the hill to it. It is the sort of town read about in novels from *Cranford* to Miss MacNaughten. Ah, Highworth as a whole! Churches and chapels, doctors' houses, Vicarage, walled gardens with pears and plums, railway station, inns and distant cemetery, old shops and winding streets. We walked down one of those narrow lanes, between garden walls, that lead under archways into the High Street. (The only way to see a town is to go down every alley and see the *backs* of the houses.) Ivy-leaved toadflax with its little purple flowers hung over the stone, an uneven line of stone-tiled roofs and slate roofs, stone and brick chimney stacks, leaded windows under eaves, all these formed a base for the church tower. There was a sound of tea being cleared away in a cottage just near us. And suddenly with a burst the bells of Highworth church rang out for Evening Service. As though called by the bells, the late sun burst out and bathed the varied roofs with gold and scooped itself into the uneven panes of old windows. Sun and stone and old brick and garden flowers and church bells. That was Sunday evening in Highworth. That was England.

A Letter

A letter to Miss Jane Boulenger, written in a very large hand with a red felt-tip pen, found by the editor in the archives of John Murray, the author's publisher.

TREEN   6/5/65

Chere M'lle,
J'ai correcté les typescripts. A
la meme temps j'ai made a list of
suitable illustrations qui je suis keeping
pour aide memoire quand nous come to
review le whole libre.
    C'est tres important pour
emphasise au le Major que les
illustrations sont tres importants,
aussi make-up. J'implore lui ne
settez anything up in type until we
discuss format et whether je suis
going to be allowed couleur aussi whether
le libre est not trop plein de
discontent & sur la meme note. Aussi
comme far ce serai possible departer
from photographs.

        Au revoir
        Seán Ó betjemán

Part Three · Metro-land

Metro-land

A script for television,* written and narrated by John Betjeman

VISION	MUSIC	COMMENTARY
Opening title sequence: Fast run from front of train, Finchley Rd/ Chesham. Subliminal superimpositions of Metro-land	*'Tiger Rag' – The Temperance Seven*	
METRO-LAND with John Betjeman	*'Build a Little Home' – Roy Fox*	
Close-ups: Metro-land brochures		JOHN BETJEMAN: Child of the First War, Forgotten by the Second, We called you Metro-land. We laid our schemes Lured by the lush brochure, down byways beckoned, To build at last the cottage of our dreams, A city clerk turned countryman again, And linked to the Metropolis by train.

*Four passages have been cut from the original script. The deleted material is summarized in square brackets. J.G.

VISION	MUSIC	COMMENTARY
Still: Quainton Rd		
Interior: Horsted Keynes Station *JB walks from bar on to platform and gets into Met. carriage*		Metro-land – the creation of the Metropolitan Railway Which, as you know, was the first steam Underground in the world. In the tunnels, the smell of sulphur was awful.
Close-up: 'Live in Metro-land' on carriage door		When I was a boy, 'Live in Metro-land' was the slogan. It really meant getting out of the tunnels into the country.
Interior of carriage *JB reading newspaper*		For the line had ambitions of linking Manchester and Paris, And dropping in at London on the way. The grandiose scheme came to nothing. But then the Metropolitan had a very good idea.
Archive film: 'A Trip on the Metro'		Look at these fields, They were photographed in 1910, from the train; 'Why not,' said a clever member of the Board, 'buy these orchards and farms as we go along, turn out the cattle, and fill the meadow land with houses?' You could have a modern home of quality and distinction – you might even buy an old one, if there was one left.

VISION	MUSIC	COMMENTARY
Close-up: JB		
Archive film		And over these mild home county acres
		Soon there will be the estate agent, coal merchant,
		Post Office, shops, and rows of neat dwellings,
		All within easy reach of charming countryside.
		Bucks, Herts and Middlesex yielded to Metro-land.
		And city men could breakfast on the fast train to London town.
Close-up: Rails		
Exterior: Baker St Station		Is this Buckingham Palace?
Interior: Chiltern Court Restaurant JB sitting at table		Are we at the Ritz? No. This is the Chiltern Court Restaurant, built above Baker Street Station, the gateway between Metro-land out there and London down there. The creation of the Metropolitan Railway.
Close-up: Brochure	*'When the Daisy Opens her Eyes' – Albert Sandler*	The brochure shows you how splendid this place was in 1913 which is about the year in which it was built. Here the wives from Pinner and Ruislip, after a day's shopping at Liberty's or Whiteley's, would sit waiting for their husbands to come up from Cheapside and Mincing Lane. While they waited they could listen to the strains of the band playing for the Thé Dansant before they took the train for home.
Mid-shot: JB		

VISION	MUSIC	COMMENTARY
Archive film: '*Leaving Baker St Station*'		Early electric – punctual and prompt.
High altitude shot: Marlborough Rd Station		Off to those cuttings in the Hampstead Hills, St John's Wood, Marlborough Road,
Train goes through		No longer stations – and the trains rush through.
JB on platform Marlborough Rd Station		This is all that is left of Marlborough Road Station. Up there the iron brackets supported the glass and iron roof. And you see that white house up there? That was where Thomas Hood
Thomas Hood house		died. Thomas Hood the poet. He wrote: 'I remember, I remember, the house where I was born', and the railway cut through his garden.
Exterior: Marlborough Rd Station		I remember Marlborough Road Station because it was the nearest station to the house where lived my future parents-in-law.
JB exits from Angus Steak House		Farewell old booking hall, once grimy brick, But leafy St John's Wood, which you served, remains,
St John's Wood houses		Fore-runner of the suburbs yet to come With its broad avenues, Detached and semi-detached villas Where lived artists and writers and military men.
		And here, screened by shrubs, Walled-in from public view,

VISION	MUSIC	COMMENTARY

		Lived the kept women.
		What puritan arms have
		    stretched within these rooms
		To touch what tender breasts,
		As the cab-horse stamped in the
		    road outside.
		
		Sweet secret suburb on the
		    City's rim,
		St John's Wood.

12 Langford Place:
'Agapemone'
		Amidst all this frivolity,
		in one place
		a sinister note is struck –
		in that helmetted house where,
		    rumour has it,
		The Reverend John Hugh
		    Smyth-Pigott lived,
		An Anglican clergyman
		whose Clapton congregation
		    declared him to be Christ,
		a compliment he accepted.
		His country house was called the
		    Agapemone –
		the abode of love –
		and some were summoned to be
		    brides of Christ.

Lilies in stained
glass windows
		Did they strew their Lord with
		    lilies?
		I don't know.
		But for some reason this house
		    has an uncanny atmosphere –
		    threatening and restless.
		Someone seems to be looking
		    over your shoulder.

House reflected in *pond – pan up to* *house*	*'The Witch of* *Endor,' ' Le Roi* *David' –* *Honegger*	Who is it?

VISION	MUSIC	COMMENTARY
Rails		Over the points by electrical traction,
Interior: Train, JB looking out of window		Out of the chimney-pots into the openness, 'Til we come to the suburb that's thought to be commonplace, Home of the gnome and the average citizen.
Exterior: Milk float, Neasden		Sketchley and Unigate, Dolcis and Walpamur.
Neasden Parade Rows of shops Houses, milkman	*'Neasden' – William Rushton*	

[*Sequence: Gladstone Park, Neasden. Mr Eric Simms speaks of the Neasden Nature Trail and bird-watching.*]

Met. tube train approaching slowly		Beyond Neasden there was an unimportant hamlet Where for years the Metropolitan didn't bother to stop. Wembley.
Still: Wembley Tower		Slushy fields and grass farms, Then, out of the mist arose Sir Edward Watkin's dream – An Eiffel Tower for London.
Still: Sir Edward Watkin		Sir Edward Watkin, Railway King, and Chairman of the Line, Thousands he thought, would pay to climb the Tower Which would be higher than the one in Paris. He announced a competition – 500 guineas for the best design.
Designs of towers		Never were such flights of Victorian fancy seen. Civil engineers from Sweden and Thornton Heath,

VISION	MUSIC	COMMENTARY
		Rochdale and Constantinople, entered designs.
		Cast iron, concrete, glass, granite and steel,
		Lifts hydraulic and electric, a spiral steam railway.
		Theatres, chapels and sanatoria in the air.
Front of brochure		In 1890 the lucky winner was
Winning design		announced.
		It had Turkish baths, arcades of shops, and Winter Gardens.
		Designed by a firm of Scots with a London office,
Still: Base of		Stewart, McLaren and Dunn.
Tower		It was to be one hundred and
Pan up		fifty feet higher
Still: Tower		Than the Eiffel Tower.
		But when at last it reached above the trees,
Still: Top of Tower		And the first stage was opened to the crowds,
		The crowds weren't there. They didn't want to come.
Still: Wide shot of		Money ran out,
tower with lake		The tower lingered on, resting and rusting
		Until it was dismembered in 1907.
Interior: Wembley		This is where London's failed
Stadium		Eiffel Tower stood. Watkin's
JB centre of pitch		Folly as it was called. Here on this Middlesex turf, and since then the site has become quite well-known.
Archive film:	*'Civic Fanfare'*	It was here,
Trumpeters and	*– Elgar*	I can just remember the
horses		excitement and the hope,
JB listening		St George's Day, 1924.

VISION	MUSIC	COMMENTARY

Archive film: Gun salute
Flags unfurling
King George V and Queen Mary
		The British Empire Exhibition at
		    Wembley,
		Opened by King George the
		    Fifth.

Exterior: Pavilions		Ah yes, those Imperial pavilions
		India, Sierra Leone, Fiji,
		With their sun-tanned sentinels
		    of Empire outside.
		To me they were more interesting
		    than

Interior: Palace of Industry		The Palaces of Industry and
		    Engineering
		Which were too like my father's
		    factory.

Exterior: Palace of Arts (today)		That was the Palace of Arts
		    where I used to wait
		While my father saw the living
		    models
		in Pears' Palace of Beauty.

Exterior: Palace of Arts (archive film)		How well I remember the Palace
		    of Arts,
		Massive and simple outside,
		Almost pagan in its sombre
		    strength,
		but inside ...

Interior: Basilica, Palace of Arts Pan up	*'Solemn Melody'* – *Walford Davies*	
JB in Basilica, Palace of Arts		This is the Basilica in the Palace of Arts. It was used for displaying the best Church art of 1924. A. K. Lawrence, Eric Gill, Mary Adshead, Colin Gill and so on. Today it's used for housing the props of the pantomime,

VISION	MUSIC	COMMENTARY
		'Cinderella on Ice' and that kind of thing. And really it's quite right because Church and Stage have always been closely connected.
Archive film: Pleasure Park	*'Masculine Women and Feminine Men'* – *Savoy Havanna Band*	
		The Pleasure Park was the best thing about the Exhibition.
King and Queen		The King and Queen enjoyed it too – There they are.
Debris and desolation of Exhibition site		Oh bygone Wembley where's the pleasure now? The temples stare, the Empire passes by. This was the grandest Palace of them all.
JB outside British Government Pavilion Close-up: Lion Zoom out		The British Government Pavilion and the famous Wembley lions. Now they guard an empty warehouse site.
Tracking shot along Oakington Rd, Wembley		But still people kept on coming to Wembley. The show-houses of the newly built estates. A younger, brighter, homelier Metro-land: 'Rusholme', 'Rustles', 'Rustlings', 'Rusty Tiles', 'Rose Hatch', 'Rose Hill', ' Rose

VISION	MUSIC	COMMENTARY
		Lea', 'Rose Mount', 'Rose Roof'.
		Each one is slightly different from the next,
		A bastion of individual taste
		On fields that once were bright with buttercups.
JB at Highfort Court, Kingsbury		Deep in rural Middlesex, the county that inspired Keats, magic casements opening on the dawn. A speculative builder here at Kingsbury let himself go, in the twenties.
High altitude shot: Harrow		And look what a lot of country there is; fields and farms between the houses, oaks and elms above the roof tops.
Archive film: 'Classic Harrow' Tube train approaching Harrow		The smart suburban railway knew its place, And did not dare approach too near the Hill.
JB at Harrow Garden Estate		Here at the foot of Harrow Hill, alongside the Metropolitan electric train, tradesmen from Harrow built in the eighties or nineties – I should think from the look of the buildings – these houses. And a nice little speculation they were. Quiet, near the railway station with their own Church and Public House; and they're named reverently after the great people of Harrow School, Drury, Vaughan and Butler.
	Harrow School Song	

VISION	MUSIC	COMMENTARY
Harrow schoolboys outside school		Valiantly that Elizabethan foundation at the top of the hill Has held the developers at bay;
Cricket match		Harrow School fought to keep this hillside green, But for all its tradition and elegance, It couldn't wholly stem The rising tide of Metro-land.
JB in Harrow		The healthy air of Harrow in the 1920s and thirties when these villas were built. You paid a deposit and eventually we hope you had your own house with its garage and front garden and back garden.
JB in Harrow		A verge in front of your house and grass and a tree for the dog. Variety created in each façade of the houses – in the colouring of the trees. In fact, the country had come to the suburbs. Roses are blooming in Metro-land just as they do in the brochures.
Close-up: Metro-land brochure *Close-ups: Houses in brochure*	*'Sunny Side of the Street' – Jack Hylton*	
Exterior: House in Harrow *Zoom in to stained glass window*		
Sequence of stained glass: sunsets, bulrushes, bluebirds, etc.		

VISION	MUSIC	COMMENTARY
Exterior: Harrow houses		Along the serried avenues of Harrow's garden villages, Households rise and shine and settle down to the Sunday morning rhythm.

[*Sequence: Sunday morning gardening, mowing lawns, washing cars, etc. to the music of Family Favourites, Rod McNeil; and 'Down by the Lazy River', The Osmonds.*]

Close-up: Fast rails

Exterior: Grims Dyke, Harrow Weald		This is Grims Dyke in Harrow Weald. I've always regarded it as a prototype of all suburban homes in southern England. It was designed by the famous Norman Shaw a century ago.
JB goes in through front door		Merrie England outside, Haunting and romantic within.
Interior: Hall, Grims Dyke, with JB		With Norman Shaw one thing leads to another. I came out of a low entrance hall into this bigger hall, and then, one doesn't know what is coming next. There's an arch and if I go up there, I'll see – goodness knows what. Let's go and look.
JB climbs stairs		There's a sense of mounting excitement. Have I strayed into a Hitchcock film?
JB arrives at dining-room		
Groups of ladies		SECRETARY: Ladies, good afternoon and welcome to the Byron Luncheon Club. I would like to give a very

VISION	MUSIC	COMMENTARY
Pan down from ceiling to groups of ladies		warm welcome to our speaker, Mrs Elizabeth Cooper.
		[*Applause.*]
		MRS COOPER:
		I would like to thank you, Madam Chairman, first of all for inviting me to this beautiful lunch, a beautiful room and bevy of beautifully dressed and beautifully hatted ladies. I think it's the most beautiful house in Harrow, one of the most interesting both architecturally and historically.
		BETJEMAN:
		Dear things, indeed it is.
Details of exterior, Grims Dyke Gables, windows, etc.		Tall brick chimney stacks Not hidden away but prominent And part of the design, Local bricks, local tiles, local timber. No façade is the same, Gabled windows gaze through leaded lights down winding lawns. It isn't a fake – it's a new practical house For a newly-rich Victorian, Strong, impressive, original.
Pool and boathouse		And yonder gloomy pool contained on May 29th 1911, the
	'Tit Willow' – *Gilbert and Sullivan*	dead body of W. S. Gilbert, Grims Dyke's most famous owner and Sullivan's partner in the Savoy Operas. After a good luncheon he went bathing with two girls, Ruby Preece and Winifred Emery. Ruby found she

VISION	MUSIC	COMMENTARY
		was out of her depth, and in rescuing her, Gilbert died, of a heart attack, here – in this pond.
Train slowly approaching Pinner		Funereal from Harrow draws the train, On, on, north-westwards, London far away, And stations start to look quite countrified.
Archive film: 'Approaching Pinner'		
		Pinner, a parish of a thousand souls, 'Til the railways gave it many thousands more.
Long shot: Train at Pinner. Pull out to show High St and Fair Roundabout and Church		Pinner is famous for its village Fair Where once a year, St John the Baptist's Day, Shows all the climbing High Street filled with stalls.
Ferris wheel, etc.		It is the Feast Day of the Parish Saint, A medieval Fair in Metro-land.
Archive film: Approaching Sandy Lodge		When I was young there stood among the fields A lonely station, once called Sandy Lodge, Its wooden platform crunched by hobnailed shoes, And this is where the healthier got out.
Archive film: Golfers	*'Golfing Love'* *– Melville Gideon*	
JB on golf course at Moor Park		One of the joys of Metro-land was the nearness of golf to London. And Moor Park, Rickmansworth, was a great attraction.

VISION	MUSIC	COMMENTARY
Prepares to drive		Now, eye on the ball Left knee slightly bent, *Slow back . . .* Missed it! [*Laughter*.]
Mid-shot: JB		Well that wasn't up to much. Perhaps the Clubhouse is more exciting.
Group drinking outside Clubhouse		Did ever Golf Club have a nineteenth hole So sumptuous as this?
Close-up: 'Reserved for Chairman' sign. Pan along signs as JB walks up to entrance		

*Interior: Hall at
Moor Park
Ceiling, murals etc.*
	*'Double
	Concerti' –
	Handel*
		Did ever Golf Club have so fine a
		    hall?
		Venetian decor, 1732.
		And yonder dome is not a dome
		    at all
		But painted in the semblance of a
		    dome;
		The sculptured figures all are
		    done in paint
		That lean towards us with so rapt
		    a look.
		How skilfully the artist takes us
		    in.

*Interior: Moor
Park*
		What Georgian wit these classic
		    Gods have heard,
		Who now must listen to the
		    golfer's tale
		Of holes in one and how I
		    missed that putt,
		Hooked at the seventh, sliced
		    across the tenth

VISION	MUSIC	COMMENTARY
		But ended on the seventeenth all square.

VISION	MUSIC	COMMENTARY
Exterior: Moor Park		Ye gods, ye gods, how comical we are! Would Jove have been appointed Captain here? See how exclusive thine Estate, Moor Park.

[*Sequence: Gate-keeper chats to lady Member in car at entrance to Estate; admits her, but turns away non-Member at barrier.*]

VISION	MUSIC	COMMENTARY
JB sitting in train carriage looking at brochure Close-up: Fast rails		Onwards, onwards, North of the border, down Hertfordshire way.
Pipe Band approaches, floats, etc.	*Pipe Band*	The Croxley Green Revels – A tradition that stretches back to 1952. For pageantry is deep in all our hearts, And this, for many a girl, is her greatest day.

[*Sequence with music: Croxley Green Revels. Procession of the Queen of the Revels. Crowd shots. The Queen is crowned. Speeches.*]

VISION	MUSIC	COMMENTARY
Archive film: Chorleywood Village		Large uneventful fields of dairy farm, Slowly winds the Chess brimful of trout, An unregarded part of Hertfordshire Awaits its fate.
		And in the heights above, Chorleywood village, Where in '89 the railway came,

VISION	MUSIC	COMMENTARY
		And wood smoke mingled with the sulphur fumes,
		And people now could catch the early train
		To London and be home just after tea.
Met. train on line – *pan left as horses* *come from under* *bridge and gallop* *across Common*		This is, I think, essential Metro-land.
		Much trouble has been taken to preserve
		The country quality surviving here –
		Oak, hazel, hawthorn, gorse and sandy tracks,
		Better for sport than farming, I suspect.
Common with *Church and School* *in background* *Children playing* *rounders in* *foreground*		Common and cricket pitch, Church School and Church, All are reminders of a country past.
		BOY: Mrs Hill, we've got eight rounders now.
Exterior: 'The *Orchard',* *Chorleywood. JB* *goes through gate* *and up to house*		JB:
		In the orchards, beyond the Common, one spring morning in 1900 a young architect, Charles Voysey, and his wife decided to build themselves a family home. I think it was the parent of thousands of simple English houses.
		'All must be plain and practical' –
		That sloping buttress wall is to counteract
Details of house		the outward thrust of the heavy slate roof.
		Do you notice those stepped tiles below the chimney-pots?

VISION	MUSIC	COMMENTARY
Details of 'The Orchard'		They're there to throw off the driving English rain, And that lead roof ridge is pinched up at the end for the same reason. Horizontal courses of red tiles in the white walls protect windows and openings. It's hard to believe that so simple and stalwart a house was built in Queen Victoria's reign.
JB at front door		Voysey liked to design every detail in his house. For instance that knocker, Voysey. A typical curious shaped handle, Voysey. And this handle or iron hinge with what seems to be his signature tune, the heart. It's there at the end of the hinge, it's here round the letterbox, it's also round the keyhole and it seems to be on the key. That's a Voysey
JB in hall		key, and in the house he did everything down to the knives and forks. The plan of the house radiates out from this hall. Extreme simplicity is the keynote. No unnecessary decoration. The balusters here for the stairs, straight verticals, giving an impression of great height to this simple hall. But as a matter of fact, it isn't a particularly high house; in fact, it's rather small. I knew Mr Voysey and I saw Mrs Voysey; they were small people and in case you think it's a large house,

VISION	MUSIC	COMMENTARY
		I'll just walk – I'm fat I know, but I'm not particularly tall – and I'll stand by the door here and you compare my height with the ledge and the door.
JB in dining-room		A round window on the garden side of the house. A typical Voysey detail. This pane which opens to let in the air from beechy Bucks, which is just on the other side of the road, over there.
Close-up: Trees. Mix to River Chess		Back to the simple life, Back to nature, To a shady retreat in the reeds and rushes Of the River Chess. The lure of Metro-land was remoteness and quiet, This is what a brochure of the twenties said: 'It's the trees, the fairy dingles and a hundred and one things in which Dame Nature's fingers have lingered long in setting out this beautiful array of trout stream, wooded slope, meadow
House names and houses at Loudwater Estate	*'Build a Little Home' – Roy Fox*	and hill-top sites. Send a postcard for the homestead of your dreams, to Loudwater Estate, Chorleywood.'
Children in swimming pool		O happy outdoor life in Chorleywood, In Daddy's swim-pool, while Old Spot looks on And Susan dreams of super summer hols,

VISION	MUSIC	COMMENTARY
		Whilst chlorinated wavelets brush the banks.
JB walks up to Len Rawle's house		O happy indoor life in Chorleywood Where strangest dreams of all are realized,
Interior: shots of organ	'Crimond' – Len Rawle	Mellifluating out from modern brick The pipe-dream of a local man, Len Rawle, For pipe by pipe and stop by stop he moved
Cutaways of pipes, effects, etc.		Out of the Empire Cinema, Leicester Square,
	'Varsity Drag' – Len Rawle	The Mighty Wurlitzer Till the huge instrument filled half his house With all its multitude of sound effects.
Stills of steam engines intercut with organ	'Chatanooga Choo Choo' – Len Rawle	Steam took us onwards, through the ripening fields, Ripe for development. Where the landscape yields
Archive film: Train to Amersham, then present day		Clay for warm brick, timber for post and rail, Through Amersham to Aylesbury and the Vale. In those wet fields the railway didn't pay, The Metro stops at Amersham today.
Mix to pool at 'High & Over', Amersham		In 1931 all Buckinghamshire was scandalized by the appearance high above Amersham of a concrete house in the shape of a letter Y. It was built for a young

VISION	MUSIC	COMMENTARY
Exterior: Various shots of 'High & Over'		professor by a young architect, Amyas Connell. They called it 'High & Over'. 'I am the home of a twentieth-century family,' it proclaimed, 'that loves air and sunlight and open country.' It started a style called Moderne – perhaps rather old-fashioned today.
Surrounding estate	*'Everything I own' – Bread*	And one day, poor thing, it woke up and found developers in its back garden. Good-bye, *High* hopes and *Over* confidence – In fact, it's probably good-bye England.
Exterior: Quainton Road Station. JB walks up steps and leans on bridge *Long shot down the line* *Quainton Road sign*		Where are the advertisements? Where the shopping arcade, the coal merchant and the parked cars? This is a part of the Metropolitan Railway that's been entirely forgotten. Beyond Aylesbury it lies in flat fields with huge elms and distant blue hills. Quainton Road Station. It was to have been the Clapham Junction of the rural part of the Metropolitan.
JB sitting on bench on Quainton Road Station		With what hopes this place was built in 1890. They hoped that trains would run down the main line there from London to the midlands and the north. They'd come from the midlands and the north rushing through here to London and a Channel Tunnel, and then on to Paris. But,

VISION	MUSIC	COMMENTARY
		alas, all that has happened is that there a line curves away to the last of the Metropolitan stations in the country in far Buckinghamshire, which was at
Still: Verney Junction		Verney Junction.
Still: Quainton Road		And I can remember sitting here on a warm autumn evening in 1929 and seeing the Brill tram
Still: Brill tram		from the platform on the other side with steam up ready to take two or three passengers through oil-lit halts and over level crossings, a rather bumpy journey to a station not far from the remote hill-top village of Brill.
JB leaning on fence at Verney Junction		
Turns to camera		The houses of Metro-land never got as far as Verney Junction.
Turns and looks down line		Grass triumphs. And I must say I'm rather glad.

Superimposed: Closing credits. Fade to black.